Migration

Migration

The Basics of Team Development

Rick Forbus, Ph.D.
Foreword by Dr. Jay Strack

Copyright © 2006 by Dr. Rick Forbus

All rights reserved. No part of this publication may be reproduced in any form, except for brief quotations in reviews, without the written permission of the publisher.

Published in the United States by Baxter Press, Friendswood, Texas.

Cover design and formatting by Anne McLaughlin, Blue Lake Design, Dickinson, Texas.

ISBN: 1-888237-62-7

Scripture taken from the Holman Christian Standard Bible, Copyright © 1999, 2000, 2002, 2003, by Holman Bible Publishers, Nashville, Tennessee. All rights reserved. Used by permission.

Printed in Canada

Dedication

The inner issues of man press especially hard against those of us who aspire to be leaders. Pride, ego, hidden agendas, materialism and a thirst for praise threaten to derail us. When they are out in public, most leaders have discovered ways to hide most of the negatives and display only the positive traits of their leadership. Sadly but inevitably, I have occasionally allowed some of these negative traits to creep into my leadership. With a clear and painful grasp of my own shortcomings, I am well aware that most of my achievements have been accomplished only by the grace of God and the honest and constructive advice from those who love me most.

That leads me to the dedication of this book. My wife and best friend, Nancy, has stuck with me through some of my stupid leadership decisions and managerial errors. Just living with me, I'm convinced, is a challenge, but she has faithfully hung in there and strongly encouraged me by her honest (and sometimes painful) advice. Every leader needs somebody who does not play the "game" and is willing to give wise counsel. As I look back on my life, I realize that some important decisions would have brought disaster if she had not been lovingly honest with me about them.

Some have said that behind every leader there is a supportive spouse. It's not that way for me. Nancy is *beside* me, leading *with* me through our journey of life. When I have done anything well, it's because she has been there as a confidante and friend.

I hope that you have someone like Nancy in your life, someone you can ask the hard questions and get honest answers. This work is dedicated to Nancy, my life-partner, friend and counselor.

Table of Contents

Acknowledgments 9
Foreword 13

1 From Goose to Formation: 15
   Mission, Purpose and Vision

2 Which Goose Leads?: 37
   Team Leaders and Roles

3 Honking and Hissing: 61
   Personal Assessments

4 Follow the Leader: 81
   Leadership 101

5 Migration: 103
   Process, Scope and Succession

6 Forecast Issues: 127
   Preferred Futuring and Strategy

7 Climate: 153
   Relationships and Corporate Citizenship

8 Honk if You Love Purpose: 173
   Team Communication

9 Cyclical Migration: 201
   Continuation and Team Building

Endnotes 215

Appendices:
   Resources 217
   About Rick Forbus 219
   About Next Level Leadership Network 221
   To Order More Copies 223

Acknowledgments

This project is the work and influence of many people. Several leaders have influenced my life along the journey. A list of all of the teachers, coaches and pastors that have had an impact on my leadership would be too numerous. Some of them, however, have not only influenced my thinking; they allowed me to make mistakes and grow toward becoming a better leader. I want to identify those people and thank them for their impact on my life.

Chuck Allen, the Chief Operating Officer of the North American Mission Board, began as a builder, layman, and visitation partner, and he became a trusted friend early in my journey. I watched God use him and shape him in incredible ways. While I watched him, I grew. He is such an encouragement to me. Next Level Leadership Network is built upon his vision and shoulders, and many leaders are encouraged today because of his belief that leadership and team development was necessary for evangelicals to fulfill their mission.

Dr. Frank Cox, my pastor, and his sweet wife Mary took Nancy and me in after we served local churches for nearly 30 years. They loved us and ministered to us. I watched Frank as a young minister as he suffered the loss of his first wife Debbie to a brain tumor. I have watched him lead, remarry, raise children and stay at North Metro First Baptist Church in Lawrenceville, Georgia, for 25 years. Leaders that stay impress me!

Dr. Jimmy Dukes, New Testament scholar and Dean of the New Orleans Baptist Theological Seminary's Extensions, has profoundly influenced my life. Jimmy not only served on my doctoral committee, but also faithfully has held the Word of God high for decades to all of his students. He has pastored and influenced many of us by his dedication to academic excellence and his shepherd's heart. Jimmy is a quiet and thoughtful leader.

Chris Goethe is a dear friend and Christian businessperson who I have watched lead from a different viewpoint than ordained career ministers. Chris has had a witness for Christ and a strong ethical stance in every business he has owned or managed. He has promoted Bible studies, men's accountability groups and general Christian ethics in the marketplace. He, too, led through the loss of his sweet Julie to cancer, raised two teenage sons alone, yet kept God first in personal and business decisions.

Through our partnership in organizational team development, David Thiel and Pat MacMillan of Triaxia Partners of Atlanta have influenced me more than they will ever know. Pat's writings, research and company reflect excellence for Fortune 50 companies as well as evangelical organizations. Much of what I facilitate in workshops and share on flipcharts I learned from Pat and David. David has mentored, coached and encouraged me to be better and better at what I do. Both men are at the top in their fields of organizational development, and they serve God and their families with spiritual wisdom and faithfulness.

My mom and dad, Kenneth and Catherine Forbus, led me to believe that nothing is impossible — and to have a sense of humor. They served for over 40 years in the same church. In their own ways, I watched both of them lead people, love them and share of themselves. They are the most generous people I have ever known. Leadership is caught not taught, and they are a testimony to that concept. The both of them modeled servanthood and strength of character. These characteristics permeated our home and now influence not only my sons and their wives, but our grandchildren as well.

Finally, books do not get to the final state of completion without edits, deletions and general syntax gymnastics. I want to thank Pat Springle and Baxter Press of Houston, Texas, for careful attention to editorial and layout issues. Pat is a great writer in his own right and shared in this project with enthusiasm. The case studies, discussion questions and other vital ingredients were his ideas.

Foreword

I've often quoted the words of the great leader and team builder Dwight Eisenhower, *"Leadership is the art of getting someone else to do something you want done because he wants to do it."*

If you're interested in forging a team that will fly in formation, everyone passionately fulfilling their assignment, willing to rotate and change duties when it's best for the team, doing whatever it takes no matter who gets the credit, then Dr. Rick Forbus' new book Migration is for you.

By exploring the creative masterpiece of nature, Rick has discovered the DNA of every migratory animal that allows it to support and protect one that is weakened or injured and that which propels it against the headwinds, storms and fierce competition of migration. Rick has put himself on a personal development plan and the results have been astonishing. I've been on the front row when he's trained some of the leading companies and organizations in the world of business and non-profits. I've been on the platform when he's recruited, trained and conducted some of the finest performances in the world of the Arts. Perhaps my favorite, I've personally watched my entire Student Leadership University staff be challenged and empowered by what Rick and the Next Level Leadership training has instilled. The Next Level Leadership training organization and principles are all over our training for middle and high school students where we teach time management, goal setting, personality skills and the Rules and Tools of Leadership.

I know of no one better to give us the tools that we need to invest in every team member to give them a sense of purpose and direction. These principles are transferable. I know because I've used some of these principles when I spoke to the Tampa Bay Buccaneers as they prepared for the play-off games and when I spoke to the coaches and scouts at the Senior Bowl. I've also shared some of the migration principles when I spoke to the remarkable engineers at NASA.

As you read these pages, you'll be challenged, stretched and motivated. The most fulfilling results will be when you implement them with your own team, whatever the assignment. You'll see lasting, meaningful relationships in real time.

Dr. Jay Strack
Studentleadership.net

CHAPTER 1

From Goose to Formation: Mission, Purpose and Vision

When attempting to establish a premise or promote some assertion, it is helpful to define terms for the topic. As we attempt to discover the truth about team development and its relation to the migration of birds, let's look at some definitions. Webster's Dictionary gives us a beginning point. It defines our key words like this:

- **Migration** is defined as a group of people, birds or fishes traveling together.

- **Migratory** refers to a group that is migrating. Here again, this would consider the migration of people, birds, fish or other herding animals. Migratory groups are characterized by their patterns of migration. **Successful migration always has a purpose and a direction, but unsuccessful migration is no more than roving or wandering.**

- **Migrate** is the act of moving from one place to another or settling in another country. It is more specific when it is an action moving from one region to another with the change of seasons, as is the case with many birds.

- A **migrant** refers to one who migrates, including the movements of people or animals. A team member or an organizational stakeholder would be considered a migrant in some situations. For instance, a person in an organization may be caught in a paradigm shift of changing values and expectations. At other times, a group member may be involved in a downsizing, restructuring or reorganization. As an organization migrates toward a new identity, the employees become migrants. This does not necessarily mean they become geographically nomadic. It means they are migrants emotionally, relationally, and psychologically.

Our discovery of migration in human behavior begins by relating the definitions of patterns of animal movement to observable patterns of team dynamics. Teams, as we will examine, have analogous and comparable characteristics to groups, crowds and herds, but the marked differences are important. These characteristics form our discussion throughout the book. Like scientists who use research techniques to study animal migration, we will examine the need for diagnostic tools to identify traits of communication and roles on teams.

If geese lived alone and had no need of collaborating to obtain their desired outcome of food and breeding habitat, then migration would not be necessary. This is also true for most people. We require interaction and migratory actions to accomplish tasks, goals, objectives, outcomes, missions, visions and destinies. Let's examine these corollaries between migratory animals and teams.

From Goose to Formation

Migration

The definition of migration — a group of people, birds or fishes traveling together — tells us that **togetherness is an irrefutable necessity** of migration and team dynamics. A sense of community is absolutely necessary. Groups, teams, flocks and herds travel **together,** whether over land, through the air or in the office. If migration requires **togetherness,** then we should examine this ingredient before proceeding.

Togetherness is an unassailable trait for groups to function effectively. A group shares at least square footage and the organizational logo, and hopefully much more: vision, mission, and strategy. On a recent trip to South Dakota, my sons and I traveled along Highway 44 headed west to cut over and eventually get on Interstate 90.

We intentionally took a different route back to Sioux Falls to shoot some video and experience the countryside and wildlife. This highway is a notable route for many Dakotans, but my sons and I were not prepared for what we saw. We are typical suburban dwellers who live outside urban centers, so we traveled to South Dakota for the space and nature of open country. Two miles from our first turn off of Highway 47 onto Highway 44 headed east, my youngest son Taylor asked, "Are those mule deer over there?" He was pointing southward at an expansive, snow-covered, harvested cornfield. I whipped the four-wheel drive vehicle over quickly to the side of the road, and we three starred in amazement at 22 mule deer migrating across a field deep in snow.

As Maclane, my oldest, snapped digital pictures and Taylor videoed this scene, here are some of things we noticed:

MIGRATION

- A large and mature doe led the way, not one of the three enormous bucks that were in the line.

- They were in a single line, rather than a more protective cluster or in several groups. By my estimation, the line stretched approximately 1600 feet.

- The group had emerged on our right from a frozen creek bed that was thick with trees on their route to the east.

- They were fully exposed to danger by taking this route.

- Interestingly, the lead doe led them through some thigh-deep snow, rather than up a few feet on ground that was not covered in snow. The few feet away, clear ground would have provided an easy path instead of each deer stumbling and struggling through the deep snow.

Here are some correlations to our teams and the concept of togetherness:

- The doe's role of leading, rather than a buck, may not be a big deal in deerdom, but it caught us off guard. She was an unexpected leader. Obviously, the deer were not individualists trying to get to a destination as 22 separate animals. They saw the need for togetherness, even though their strategy seemed odd. These deer chose to be together to get somewhere. Each mule deer was large and mature enough to go it alone, but they chose to cooperate to get to their destination.

- They traveled in a single line. Three adult humans questioned their methodology! If I were a mule deer, I would have tried a different plan. We will talk later about purpose, mission and vision. I cannot comment on the reason that these 22 chose to form a single line rather than sub groups, task forces or gender sets. The bottom line, as with virtually all migratory paths, is that they chose to go **together.**

- The deer had made a choice not to stay at Point A but to travel to Point B. I wish we could have observed how, why and when they communicated the plan to each other to get up and move. Scientists tell us that migratory animals instinctively move as a creative design component. The basic point here is that together they moved from Point A to Point B. I guess they could have considered possible scenarios, and each deer could have moved when and how it chose to migrate. But no matter how they made their decision, they chose to move together.

- The dangerous route they chose was intriguing. I live in Georgia, where seeing two to four deer moving together is normal, but only occasionally, one might see a small herd, usually at dusk. In Georgia, white tail deer in heavy forested areas are like stealth aircraft. They move quietly and in heavy vegetation. Only once or twice in my entire life of watching deer have I ever seen more than six or seven moving out in the open in broad daylight. What parallel do I conclude from this? The route chosen by these 22 deer in South Dakota was worth the danger. The mule deer chose instinctively to get up together and move

MIGRATION

across an open, deeply snowed field in broad daylight to get where they were going. The risk was worth the danger. Of course, they lived in one of the most under-populated areas in America, and it was after hunting season had ended. Maybe their groupthink in the creek bed led them to take the most direct, yet the most dangerous, route. This parallels a topic we will explore called "healthy divergence and the risk of interdependence."

- Our last observation is the scene of each deer struggling in the deep snow, following the leader hoof print by hoof print. Remember, only a few feet away they could have enjoyed clear terrain where the snow had been blown away, and they could have walked much more easily. I know this because days earlier the three of us had walked across similar terrain and through deep snow. Each of us had sought clear land rather than take the risk and intense labor of walking in deep snow. Why did the herd of deer follow this doe along a far more difficult path? Why did the other stronger deer, the bucks, not move to the front and provide deeper and strategic footprints for the others? Why did the deer robotically follow this way, rather than choosing an easier trail? Unless you hold a PhD in Animal Husbandry or you have studied the behaviors of deer a great deal more than I have, we can only assume that they chose to follow the lead doe. The learning for human groups is this: some people just follow without knowing why the path was chosen. Many groups just robotically line up, step where they are shown to step, and co-exist in a basic state of togetherness.

Migration can also be observed in the context of chemistry as the shifting of position of one or more atoms within a molecule, or the movement of ions toward an electrode. Move with me from science to team dynamics and discover this parallel. Every organization has group chemistry. We will investigate this later in the chapter on relationships, but at this point, let me suggest some things to build a bridge to our ultimate destination. Geese, deer, ducks and humans sometimes travel toward synergistic results when migrating. The reason I use the word *sometimes* is that many times groups, especially humans, end at *an unspecified* (and often unwanted) *result,* not a synergistic, well-defined and desired outcome. As we shall find, team migration is powerful when it flies on the wings of well-defined goals that receive lift by a clear, common and compelling purpose.

MIGRATORY

Migratory actions have observable and predictable characteristics, tendencies and outcomes. Remember what Webster told us: the word "migratory" refers to a group that is traveling together, including the migration of people, birds, fish or other herding animals. Migratory groups are characterized by the nature of their migration. How groups migrate, united by their togetherness, defines their signature. In other words, groups are defined by their migration markings. When we get into the chapter on diagnostic tools and assessments, we will delve into traits, tendencies, genetics and personality issues. Here, it will suffice just point out some team issues:

- Individuals, and their behaviors that span the continuum of trait descriptors, will form a sense of togetherness around their purpose, mission and vision.

- The antithesis is also true. Individuals will not form into teams without a clearly defined and compelling purpose, mission and vision. Individuals have a tendency to stay confined to mere groups, herds or crowds without a defining purpose, mission, goal or vision.

- Because a goose is on the ground with other geese does not necessarily mean that the group can begin migrating together. In the same way, receiving your paycheck from the same business account as others does not mean you function in a migratory fashion toward a common, prevailing purpose. And volunteering in an organization and coexisting with others that have the same "t-shirt" does not mean you will migrate together to fulfill a corporate purpose or vision.

- Sociologists have identified a phenomenon called "the psychology of crowd." Migratory groups have discernable characteristics. For at least a couple of thousand years, people on this planet have been engaged in a lively (and occasionally deadly) debate over the **collective wisdom** of crowds. Crowds, groups and organizations are interchangeable when it comes to their psychological tendencies. In an expansive view, crowds could be defined as a family, a company unit, a task force team, a congregation or even a one-time gathering. **Are crowds smart or stupid?**

- Sometimes crowds act stupidly when they engage in unjust wars, burning witches, drowning heretics, rioting and other acts of mindless destruction. This suggests that the collective IQ of the masses may be somewhat limited, or unfortunately, unintelligent.

- Sometimes, however, crowds act brilliantly. Democracy is based on the idea that the collective intelligence of the voting public is better at deciding who should govern than the single, narrow mind of a dictator.

- However, the popularity of democratic choice is not necessarily always a reflection of the collective intelligence of a crowd. There has to be something greater than just the democratic framework to allow crowds to become synergistic teams. There has to be something beyond popular vote or consensus. The popularity of ANYTHING — movies, books, music, art, pizza...you name it — is hardly ever an indication of its quality. In fact, most times the opposite is true.

- Migratory tendencies have little to do with democratic votes or authoritarian edicts. Popularity is certainly not the answer to building a sustainable "buy in" to migration toward synergistic purpose. Alexis de Tocqueville famously pointed this out over 150 years ago. He discovered that American culture is largely guided by a general "contempt for excellence" that continually threatens to drag everything down to the lowest common denominator. Or does it? After all, America has the greatest universities, companies, hospitals and athletes in the world, so we must be doing something right. But just because a country, organization or group has intellect, finances, talents, gifts and power does not guarantee synergy. Actually, Tocqueville discovered that when left alone without purpose, crowds drift downwards away from excellence and synergistic results.

- James Surowieki wrote in *The New Yorker* business section that "crowds are decidedly more intelligent and reliable decision-makers than most of us would ever suspect." He recounts the story of British scientist, Francis Galton, who, in 1906, observed a contest at the local county fair to guess the weight of an ox after it was slaughtered and dressed. Galton was interested in what the AVERAGE PERSON'S guess would be, because he wanted to prove that the average "voter" was an unreliable judge of just about everything. Instead, he discovered that when 787 guesses were averaged, the result came within a pound of the actual weight. The crowd's judgment was impeccable. From this observation, Surowieki surmised: Masses of minds working together can be uncannily accurate when it comes to answering certain types of questions and solving problems.[1]

- The crucial difference between a DUMB CROWD with a "herd mentality" and a SMART CROWD that arrives at intelligent collective decisions is the level of diversity and interdependence of the individuals in the group. The BOTTOM LINE is this: Diversity and interdependence are important because the best collective decisions are the product of disagreement and contest, not consensus or compromise. Migratory actions include divergence, disagreement, discussions and shared desires.

From Goose to Formation

- Around the lake where I walk, I have heard a lot of honking from the geese that live there. It may be a stretch, but I believe their honking displays their divergence, even though they still take flight together and arrive on the lake in unified way. I just believe a strong blend of individuality and unity is the way of life for geese, and it should be for humans, too. Celebrate a little group divergence and healthy conflict, and then move together in a migration toward a common prevailing purpose.

Migrate

"Migrate" is the act of moving from one place to another or settling in another country. When people are employed, enlisted or decide to sign up to join a group, they are in essence agreeing to migrate toward an outcome. The group always expects a result — but whether the results are clearly defined is another issue. It would be difficult for geese to migrate from Canada to the Gulf States if there was not some defining outcome that "lifted" them upward and onward.

We will talk later about sustainable goals and outcomes, but when an organization migrates toward purpose, it should strive for endurance, not quick, shallow wins. Clint Courtney never made it into the Baseball Hall of Fame. In fact, it is very doubtful that his picture ever appeared on any baseball cards. He was not even a legend in his own time. He was only a memory maker for his family and a few die-hard fans. Clint played catcher for the Baltimore Orioles in the 1950s. During his career, he earned the nickname of "Scrap Iron," because he was hard, weathered, and tough. Old Scrap broke no records — only bones. He had little power with his bat or speed on the base paths. As for grace and style, he made the easiest play look rather difficult. Nevertheless, armed with mitt and mask, Scrap Iron never flinched from any challenge.

Opposing batters often missed the ball and caught his shin. Their foul tips nipped his elbow. Runners fiercely plowed into him, spikes first, as he defended home plate. Though often doubled over in agony and flattened in a heap of dust, Clint Courtney never quit. Invariably, he would slowly get up, shake off the dust, punch the pocket of his mitt once or twice, and nod to his pitcher to throw another one. The game would go on, and Courtney— scarred, bruised, clutching his arm in pain — was determined to continue. He resembled a P.O.W. with tape, splints, braces, and other kinds of paraphernalia that wounded people wear. Some made fun of him — calling him a masochist or insane, but others remember him as a true champion — a man with the capacity to endure. Yes, Clint Courtney was a man of endurance, a person with the ability to migrate toward his purpose in life.

Like Clint Courtney, the Ancient Greeks knew about endurance. The Greeks had a unique race in their Olympic games. Each runner in the race carried a torch. The winner was not the man who finished first, but rather the runner who finished with his torch still lit. Imagine what the world would be like today if our culture did not define success by achievement, but by the capacity to endure or sustain our migration. Success for groups is discovered as they migrate together toward a common purpose and overwhelming outcome. The purpose sustains them and lends endurance to the migration. A clearly defined purpose is the proverbial torch, and keeping it lit is a team task. Geese even honk encouragement to each other as they migrate toward their goal.

Migrant

A "migrant" refers to one who migrates, and implies movement of persons or animals. A migrant worker travels from field to field, region to region, and his journey is dependent on seasonal changes. Migrants are the cogs and wheels of the machinery called "migration." Without migrants, there would be no migration. Geese, deer, ducks and humans become migrants when they migrate toward some desired outcome, and one is a migrant only when caught up in some migratory path headed for some purposeful outcome.

Just because a migrant intentionally moves from place to place does not presuppose that the movement is nomadic and without purpose. As we look at this idea in light of team development, movement toward mission must be well defined and flexible. Organizational seasons march forward just like the seasons that stimulate the migration of geese. The migrants must understand the fluidity of situations and the change of seasons. Purpose keeps migrants laser-locked into the migration itself, no matter where it takes them.

Team Purpose and Individuality

As people find themselves in various types of organizations, some important choices precede team synergism. An individual has to make these choices:
1. Will I carry out my work assignment with as little interaction with others as possible?

2. Will I limit my interaction to only those situations that help me succeed?

3. Will I take full individual responsibility for my actions and my performance?

4. Will I present my talents, gifts and labors to accomplish a strong, clear, prevailing purpose?

5. Will I perceive my work as something that interconnects with others?

6. Will I sense a mutual accountability to the continental purpose of the organization and do my best whenever possible?

7. Will I lend exceptional effort to the purpose because of the synergistic team sharing of the vision?

The answers to these questions either hinder or leverage the movement from single employees or volunteers to the formation of a team. A lone goose that flies into an existing flock has to bridge his individualism toward togetherness. Leaders must exhibit the ability to link individual group members to a powerful purpose, mission or vision. Leadership is not management. In fact, I am not sure you can manage people to form a team. You can give them a logo, team jersey and mission statement. You can even make them memorize the mission statement, but that does not mean they are buying in. Verbal assent certainly is not the same as lending exceptional effort to the common purpose. It may be impossible to manage people to buy into a compelling purpose. Just look at the definitions and synonyms of the word "manage":

- Run
- Direct
- Administer
- Supervise
- Deal with
- Control
- Cope

We all can cite cases where people did not buy into a corporate strategy or overarching purpose simply because they were told that they should. For example, when we're shopping, it's obvious that many people who wait on us certainly do not embrace the corporate values and purpose of the company that made the product or the store selling it. The same is true in service organizations, charitable groups and religious denominations. Quite often, employees do not embrace and practice the common purpose of the larger organization. Management, discipline and threats do not really solve this issue. Let me illustrate this.

Let's Get Rid of Management

People don't want to be managed...they want to be led.

Whoever heard of a world manager?
World leader, yes.
Educational leader, yes.
Political leader, yes.
Religious leader, yes.

Community leader, yes.
Scout leader, yes.
Labor leader, yes.
Business leader, yes.

They lead. They don't manage. The carrot always wins over the stick. Ask your horse. You can lead him to water, but you can't manage him to drink. You feed him salt and make him thirsty; that's motivation. If you want to manage somebody, manage yourself. Do that well, and you'll be ready to stop managing…and start leading.

In his book, *The Performance Factor,* Pat MacMillan states these things are needed for common purpose:

Purpose must be…

- **Clear — "Understand It"** — Each group member, volunteer or employee understands it and can, to some degree explain what "it" is.

- **Relevant — "Want It"** — Stakeholders believe their purpose is relevant to the world they live in.

- **Significant — "Worth It"** — Team members see purpose as significant enough to invest their time, talent, cooperation and effort toward it.

- **Achievable — "Believe It"** — Stakeholders see purpose as lofty enough that it is worth synergistic effort, but not so nebulous or high-level that members cannot embrace it and believe it is attainable.

- **Urgent — "Time is an Issue"** — Anything worth great amounts of cooperation and efforts are worth specificity in deadlines. Team purpose must have time allotments and succession markers to allow it to be dynamic and measurable. The absence of specific time constraints and markers will lead to less-than-synergistic effort. The same would be true to ask runners to run without giving them a time to beat as their goal.[2]

In most scenarios, individuals have trouble giving a large amount of emotional currency, exceptional exertion and cooperation to achieve a poorly defined purpose. I share often and with much passion that leaders should celebrate their purpose frequently with their teams. I find there is an indisputable and widespread organizational weakness: the lack of a consistently clarified purpose. Every time leaders stand before a team or in front of a large gathering, they need to celebrate their purpose. Leaders should imagine they are holding up a simple sign for all to see each time they interact with their people. Of course, words laced with clarity and purpose will suffice when stating purpose.

Sometimes leaders assume that carefully crafted mission statements are enough to keep the purpose before the stakeholders, but just because a vision statement has been written and hung in the front foyer or on the boardroom wall does not mean that everyone gets it. Surprisingly, many top-level leaders think their people have internalized the corporate purpose simply because they have had a wordsmith construct one. Some think that because the annual off-site retreat was designed to write the mission statement, the team will celebrate it. One team had their mission statement printed on one side of a business card-sized, laminated handout. On the other side were their core values. On a pre-workshop visit, I picked up one in the information center and began to study it. I kept it in my pocket for a few weeks to be prepared to help the team work on their purpose in a workshop. As we got neck deep into calibrating the differences in their declared values and their real values, one young staff member spoke up. He asked, "Where did you get this set of values that we are working from here?" I proudly went into my pocket and revealed the laminated card with their mission statement and core values. He said, "May I see that?" When I handed it to him, he told me that this card was produced nearly ten years before. The tenured staff looked equally surprised. I was embarrassed. I had structured the entire day around these values and was guiding the team to calibrate purpose and discover what was real and what was just declared as their values and purpose.

The defining teaching points that day were these:

- The message on the printed card was not only outdated; it was still being circulated without having any significance.

- The scary thing was that naive organizational coaches like me and a few other folks maybe looking at antiquated, irrelevant statements for clues about what this enterprise valued.

- It was being circulated, even if unintentionally, for anyone to read.

- The leaders were not aware that it was still out for public consumption.

- Although the core values and the mission statement printed on the card looked well thought out and probably took hours of groupthink, nobody was doing them!

This serendipitous discovery changed our course for the team workshop, but the group learning was invaluable. From this new, fresh starting point, we worked through the team's *declared* values and what were *real* values. We listed what were assumed values and then clarified their purpose. We then listed what was really going on. This workshop was a model for all organizational teams: the discovery of what was really happening dictates real values. From there, this team spent some important time defining and simplifying their purpose.

Purpose is the nucleus of organizational or ministry activity. Purpose, mission and core values are the focus of high-performance organizations. Until a group of stakeholders define a common purpose, the activities, calendar dates and expenditures may not reflect their purpose. Do not put anything on a calendar that does not lift purpose higher. Do not fund any idea that does not boost purpose. The mule deer had such a compelling purpose that they lined up behind a lead doe and efficiently marched toward their desire outcome with no wasted movement nor wasted energy. These migrating animals were an organizational team, and their actions reflected their common purpose. With a clear, compelling purpose, there would not be a glut of "feel good" activities on the calendar that nobody had the fortitude to stop doing, and activities would be added only when they were needed to propel purpose. There would be no sacred cows that somebody started years ago that could not be stopped because of the political fallout. Like the mule deer and the Canada geese, each step and each down stroke of the organization's daily activity calendar would be filled with common, compelling and clear purpose!

MIGRATION

CASE STUDY #1

A very large and very traditional church called a new pastor. He was young and full of ideas. He inherited a large and tenured staff, and some staff members had been there well over twenty years. In his later years, the former pastor allowed the organization to drift from the core values that long ago defined its compelling purpose. From my observation, the mission had shifted, but the activities and strategies had stayed the same. The long-term staff celebrated the former "glory days", while the new pastor and his new hires were perplexed. The team workshops resembled Australian Rules football. The tenured staff would run the ball of the former purpose a few yards, and then the new pastor and his new team would pick it up and run for a while. My job as an organizational coach was to question and facilitate this "game," while trying to get everybody to discover a common purpose and begin building a plan that would boost that purpose.

DISCUSSION QUESTIONS

1. What hindrances to this team being synergistically together do you observe?

2. Have you experienced anything like this? Explain.

3. If you were the coach, what would be your first step in helping this team find common purpose?

4. When should an old activity, program or paradigm go away?

5. Give a sample plan of action that would assist this team in discovering best practices that only propel common purpose.

6. What criteria should be used to determine if a program or activity should be sustained?

7. When does the overarching purpose need to be reassessed and recalibrated?

CHAPTER 2

WHICH GOOSE LEADS?: TEAM LEADERS AND ROLES

*M*igrating geese and ducks are remarkable. As they shift roles so that a fresh, strong bird replaces a tired one at the front of the V, how do they determine whose turn it is to lead? Since creation, they instinctively have practiced shared roles and interdependence. It seems that they have little difficulty with teamwork — something that humans struggle with. What are these migratory birds actually doing, and why are they doing it? A lot of academic research speaks of this phenomenon. One site describes it this way:

> *The "V" formation is a formation used for flying farther. The lead bird breaks the air and stirs up updrafts at the other birds' wing tips. In the updrafts, behind the birds, the birds can get 70% more distance. The outer position gives better view ahead. Lead birds change often, not because of social orders, but because of fatigue. The geese stay in the "V" shape because misalignment on drafts increase the workload.*[3]

MIGRATION

Migratory birds know to form a flock rather than fly separately. God, in His infinite power and creativity, placed in each bird the desire to join others in a flock. This formation may provide protection, companionship or team synergy — probably all three. Scientists tell us that the migratory plan would not succeed if geese or ducks took off singularly to the desired destination. They would take too long and miss their breeding season, and each bird would fail to arrive because of the lack of stamina. They need each other to survive and thrive.

As we look at roles on teams and how they interplay with other characteristics, let me use the insights about geese to draw more parallels with our teams.

1. **Why would single birds hatched by individual mothers decide to form a group to migrate?** To accomplish their purpose, geese instinctively travel toward their ultimate migratory destination in groups to increase stamina and save time.

2. **Why were they created to form a "V" and not any other formation choices?** The research says that the lead bird breaks the air to make flying easier for the other birds.

3. **Why do they stay in a "V" the entire route?** The research also says that each stroke of the bird in front causes an updraft. In other words, the front bird cuts the air and lifts the next two birds to make flying easier and more efficient. His down stroke causes a slight vacuum, and his up stroke causes a lift. The "V" is the only shape that would allow for this to occur for each and every bird in formation behind the lead bird.

4. **How much further can they go in formation like this?** The research says that each bird, when flying in these constant updrafts, can fly 70% further than they could fly individually. Remarkably, many species fly hundreds of miles every year, instinctively knowing that drafting off each other will take them the distance that they could not travel alone.

5. **Does the lead bird have more stamina than all the other birds?** Lead birds cannot endure the entire trip in the front, so they often change positions. They do not change because of positional authority or because of tenured service. Apparently, all the birds lead at some point on the journey! They simply change leaders because of fatigue. The leaders do not have a political agenda, an underlying motive or longer wings. They change because they each cannot complete the journey alone, nor can they travel it in the front the entire way.

6. **How do they decide which geese are in the flock that travels together?** Like me, you have probably noticed that several flocks often fly overhead in the same direction. How do they form their distinct teams? Research tells us, "Families gather together to form flocks." As the time for migration approaches, they gather their families together and begin their journey.[4]

7. **Is there another purpose for this formation?** The flock depends on the leader to be able to see for the team. Although the leader experiences wind resistance and the fatigue, he also has the best view. The leader can spot water, food and danger.

MIGRATION

8. **What common purpose has drawn so many species of migratory birds faithfully to pursue this pilgrimage for thousands of years?** Scientists who study the connection between migratory birds and rice production have observed:

Some geese stop for short rests in the Dakotas, the Midwest and other prairies. But, some fly thousands of miles without stopping! Among the most popular destinations of these snowbirds are the rice fields of the United States. These states include Arkansas, California, Louisiana, Mississippi, Missouri and Texas. Rice farmers, with the cooperation of conservationist groups, have turned their rice fields, which in winter would normally lay unused, into a wetlands habitat for migrating geese. Here, in the flooded rice fields, geese thrive in their usual conditions, surrounded by shallow, vegetation-rich water. The rice straw left after harvest provides shelter and protection. Leftover rice grain, weeds and water insects offer an abundant and nutritious food supply. The arrangement is also advantageous for the rice farmer. The traffic of the birds help the rice straw decompose more quickly and the birds eat weeds and weed seeds. The birds' droppings are beneficial as fertilizer.[5]

Apparently, their common purpose not only includes intermediate steps along the way, but they have a wider impact on the land where they fly. As we will see later in this chapter, the journey and the roles are as important as the project, mission or purpose before us.

9. **Why does misalignment create less efficient travel for geese?** Just as a NASCAR driver only benefits from drafting if he stays a few feet behind the car in front of him, a goose needs to stay perfectly positioned to gain the proper alignment for maximum uplift of draft. If the goose is just a little out of position, the draft off the goose in front will not be as efficient. The greatest benefit occurs when birds —and team members — are perfectly aligned. The slightest angle of misalignment will cause the efficiency to diminish. For this reason, individual team members must commit to be positioned perfectly, not only to benefit from each other's differences and strengths, but also with the corporate purpose. When a team of interdependent people align themselves with the desired outcome of the task or vision, no efficiency is lost. Conversely, if a team member chooses to misalign through lack of effort, poor competencies or a defective character, team synergy is lost and no uplift occurs. For this reason, team leaders should frequently clarify purpose and attempt to create alignment with the team.

Team and Organizational Roles

One of the most emotionally charged discussions I encounter in working with groups is on the topic of roles. The lack of understanding one's role can bring insecurity, disempowerment and wasted effort. Most often, misunderstandings stem from a few common problems: (1) lack of clarity of overall purpose, (2) unclear team assignments and (3) the risk of interdependence.

MIGRATION

We all have encountered the volatility of misunderstanding a role even within our families. Husbands and wives sometimes struggle when roles in the home are not clear. This problem could surface in disciplining children, managing money or making household decisions. On teams, one or more people in the organization did not understand their role, or someone thought their role was more important than someone else's. Roles intersect with basic human feelings, so it is important to be considerate of others' needs. This story illustrates the point:

During my second month of college, our professor gave us a pop quiz. I was a conscientious student and had breezed through the questions until I read the last one: "What is the first name of the woman who cleans the school?" Surely, this was some kind of joke. I had seen the cleaning woman several times. She was tall, dark-haired and in her 50s, but how would I know her name? I handed in my paper, leaving the last question blank. Just before class ended, one student asked if the last question would count toward our quiz grade. "Absolutely," said the professor. "In your careers, you will meet many people. All are significant. They deserve your attention and care, even if all you do is smile and say "hello." I've never forgotten that lesson. I also learned her name was Dorothy.

This professor had outstanding, teaching and leadership skills, and he taught a lesson that is vital to many leaders. Too many leaders feel comfortable and powerful only because they hold the "position." Far too many of them lead from the security of their box on the organizational chart. This professor taught something that is not usually found on exams or in academic literature: he taught the importance of roles. Without Dorothy's tireless and thankless work, the students and the professors would not have been able to fulfill their roles in comfort and without distraction. She brought synergy and completeness to this academic institution. Her role made the students' and the professors' academic experience more enjoyable and complete. One senior pastor was heard saying repeatedly that his staff existed to fulfill *his* vision, but the proper understanding of the importance of roles launches every team into a high level of accomplishing the *corporate* purpose. Pat MacMillan says particular characteristics of roles must be understood, including:

1. Dividing the task into roles is the strategy for leveraging the results.

2. Interdependence and role clarity become critically important when the task is divided…understanding my and others' roles is critical.

3. Role possibilities include: *clear, confused,* and *chaotic.*

4. Managing our interdependence suggests we need to master role boundaries, role attitudes, and role differences.

5. Teams need to learn the concept of *personal responsibility* and *mutual accountability.*[6]

Some leaders prefer to wear masks instead of defining roles. The mask is designed to project power and authority, but it hinders the leader from being honest, humble, and effective in building up others. These leaders are proud of their positions, and they enjoy the trappings of power, such as the big office or their name printed in an organizational box that is higher than others.

Leveraging roles comes when leaders realize that the purpose, which is made of tasks, is divided among the various roles of the team. Realizing the importance of others and their roles is important. This true story is a great example of risk-taking in the area of human behavior:

One night, at 11:30 p.m., an older African American woman was standing on the side of an Alabama highway trying to endure a lashing rainstorm. Her car had broken down and she desperately needed a ride. Soaking wet, she decided to flag down the next car. A young white man stopped to help her, which was generally unheard of in those conflict-filled 1960s. The man took her to safety, helped her get assistance and put her into a taxicab. She seemed to be in a big hurry, but she wrote down his address and thanked him. Seven days went by and a knock came on the man's door. To his surprise, a giant console color TV was delivered to his home. A special note was attached. It read: "Thank you so much for assisting me on the highway the other night. The rain drenched not only my clothes, but also my spirits. Then you came along. Because of you, I was able to make it to my dying husband's bedside just before he passed away... God bless you for helping me and unselfishly serving others."

Sincerely,
Mrs. Nat King Cole

Some leaders preach on servanthood, selflessness and caring for others, but they have trouble practicing it in the every day organizational life of ministry. In

WHICH GOOSE LEADS?

I Corinthians 12, Paul tells us that all of us have God-given roles to play. He wrote:

Now there are different gifts, but the same Spirit. There are different ministries, but the same Lord. And there are different activities, but the same God is active in everyone and everything. (verses 4-6)

Defining roles should be a frequent activity of staff meetings and volunteer training. Many times in strategy meetings, purpose can be well defined and process may be calibrated, but role clarity is ignored. MacMillan says, "Dividing the task into roles is the strategy for leveraging the results."[7] Authoritarians do not recognize the importance of dividing the tasks and leveraging roles. Those who lead from a dictatorial position often tire in pursuit of their purpose and stop short of accomplishing the goal because the journey is too tough to travel alone. Just like the geese, leveraging the role of others and drafting off their energy can carry a leader farther and higher. In I Corinthians 12, Paul goes on to say,

A manifestation of the Spirit is given to each person to produce what is beneficial:
To one is given a message of wisdom through the Spirit,
To another, a message of knowledge by the same Spirit,
To another, faith by the same Spirit,
To another, gifts of healing by the one Spirit,
To another, the performing of miracles,
To another, prophecy,
To another, distinguishing between spirits,
To another, different kinds of languages,
To another, interpretation of languages.

MIGRATION

But one and the same Spirit is active in all these, distributing to each as He wills. (verses 7-11)

When it comes to experiencing strong, synergistic roles on a team, some leaders talk and preach about it but do not practice it. One senior leader of a large church had me come explain to him and his executive team about team development, which includes the leveraging of roles and dividing the tasks that lead to the fulfillment of purpose. He loved the material, and after the first workshop, he was complimentary. However, he privately shared some concern about dividing the task. He was anxious that he might have to become a follower at times and not remain the leader. My explanation was that biblically he was the under shepherd of God and is called to shepherd the church, but the description of roles in I Corinthians 12 is the biblical template for leading a team. He was afraid he would have to give away too much power. He was infatuated with power as much as was he insecure about what could happen if team members were allowed to operate completely in their giftedness and contribute to the decisions and success of the team. Nevertheless, God worked in this man's heart. Several workshops and coaching experiences later, he fully enjoyed the power of leveraging roles and drafting off the others on the team.

In I Corinthians 12, Paul finishes the thought concerning roles in ministry:

Now you are the body of Christ, and the individual members of it. And God has placed these in the church: First apostles, second prophets, third teachers, next miracles, then gifts of healing, helping, managing, various kinds of languages.

WHICH GOOSE LEADS?

Are all apostles? Are all prophets? Are all teachers?
Do all do miracles?
Do all have gifts of healing? Do all speak in languages?
Do all interpret?
But desire the greater gifts. And I will show you an even better way. (verses 27-31)

Surprisingly, some Christian leaders think they are the total package and need to handle all of the roles mentioned in this passage, but whether the organization is large or small, clarifying and leveraging roles is necessary. I spoke with a very innovative church planter in one of the world's largest cities about this topic. He, by the way, really understands this concept. He told me how he was the only paid staff member of a flourishing church start. He believed that he was to treat all of the volunteers who wanted to be a part of the ministry as non-paid employees. He helped clarify their purpose and often celebrated the church's mission. He allowed them to work within their giftedness and take leadership roles in projects when their gifts were stronger than his. For instance, he told me of a person who was once in a gang that now headed up outreach and ministry for urban gangs. The pastor not only found himself *behind* this man in the "V" formation, he many times was in the very back, functioning as a follower and learner in this area of ministry.

When the task is divided among several people, interdependence and role clarity become critically important. Each person needs to grasp his own role and the roles of each person on the team. When a leader is afraid to let others lead, the collective brilliance and power of what is taught in I Corinthians 12 is lost. Synergy is discovered in the interplay of roles. When individuals are working together toward a common purpose, and the various tasks are divided, the relationship of their roles is crucial.

As we continue to examine roles, look at a few other biblical passages that celebrate this team concept.

Exodus 18:17-19 speaks to team synergy and the concept of shared roles in an overwhelming ministry situation:

"What you are doing is not good," Moses' father-in-law said to him. "You will certainly wear out both yourself and these people who are with you, because the task is too heavy for you. You can't do it alone."

Jethro, Moses' father-in-law, took a relationship risk to make an organizational suggestion. Moses was the positional leader and the functional expert. Moses had his name in the top box on the organizational chart, but Moses was not practicing the principles of team dynamics. He was trying to do it all alone. Jethro said that this thing that you are doing, Moses, is not good. Jethro predicted pending burnout if Moses did not change his leadership style. Not only did Jethro anticipate Moses' exhaustion, but he also warned him that the people were tired of this style of leadership.

When modern leaders choose to lead with a top-down style, they risk burnout, and so do those following them. Sometimes followers openly rebel, and sometimes they just fade away. When leaders fail to empower, delegate and celebrate the different roles of the team, followers and team members can easily become disengaged.

WHICH GOOSE LEADS?

Exodus 18:19-21 continues to clarify this concept of roles. In this passage, notice how the proper use of roles can leverage a common purpose through the interplay of individual responsibility and mutual accountability.

"Now listen to me; I will give you some advice, and God be with you. You be the one to represent the people before God and bring their cases to Him. Instruct them about the statues and laws, and teach them the way to live and what they must do. But you should select from all the people able men, God-fearing, trustworthy, and hating bribes. Place [them] over the people as officials of thousands, hundreds, fifties, and tens."

Jethro's leadership plan was a good one. Straightforwardly, he tells this larger-than-life, highly respected leader, Moses, "I've got some advice for you." He told Moses to understand the roles needed to overcome his gigantic task of ministering to multitudes of needy people. He advised Moses to be the functional expert, or keeper of the vision, but to select and train others to handle tasks. Moses was to coach and mentor others to use their gifts and roles to complete the tasks. Jethro gave Moses advice about the skills and character of those he would select. Jethro also had an organizational plan that included management over thousands, hundreds, fifties and tens. The roles of these team members were to be directed by Moses as they connected with each other. In other words, like a runner in a relay handing off a baton to another runner, these leaders were to hand off responsibilities as directed by Moses. With this approach, Moses did not have to sit and minister to such a large crowd alone. He could leverage the roles of others to complete the task better than before!

MIGRATION

This account in Exodus provides more leadership and management insights for Moses and us. Look at verses 22-27:

"They should judge the people at all times. Then they can bring you every important case but judge every minor case themselves. In this way you will lighten your load, and they will bear [it] with you. If you do this, and God [so] directs you, you will be able to endure, and also all these people will be able to go home satisfied." Moses listened to his father-in-law and did everything he said. So Moses chose able men from all Israel and made them leaders over the people [as] officials of thousands, hundreds, fifties, and ten. They judged the people at all times; the hard cases they would bring to Moses, but every minor case they would judge themselves. Then Moses said goodbye to his father-in-law, and he journeyed to his own land.

Jethro did not just have a plan; he had a very *detailed* plan that included the risk of interdependence. The risk was that Moses now had to trust others to do what he had previously done alone. This is tough transition for some leaders, but not for Moses. He was open and willing to respect his father-in-law's plan. Jethro suggested that the chosen men bring the major cases to Moses, but everything else should be handled by the others fulfilling their roles according to their giftedness and skill sets. This plan is so rich and powerful that it's easy to think it was just written last week in one of the many modern leadership and management books, but it's God's ancient and proven plan to allow the various roles to fulfill the greater desired outcome.

Which Goose Leads?

Jethro did not just pitch a plan that dealt with the hard issues of the ministry. He gave a plan that would include the soft issues as well. His plan acknowledged the strain on Moses and the discouragement of the people, and it provided a way for Moses to endure and for the people to experience satisfaction.

He told Moses that if he accepted this plan to allow the roles to play out synergistically, the needs of the people would be met. That was the bottom line; the people were fulfilled and blessed. It also appears that Moses agreed to Jethro's advice with a great attitude. He said his goodbyes, and then Jethro and Moses parted ways. Wow! I wish all of our interdependence and organizational changes went as well as this. Wouldn't it be great if positional leaders would take some advice from an historical leader like Moses? In Sid Kemp's book entitled *Project Management Demystified*, he defines roles this way:"A defined set of responsibilities in relation to a project, work environment, or social situation."[8]

Kemp defines a project manager's role specifically as it fits in a team environment. He also shows how it corresponds to an overall organizational purpose and team task. He writes:

The Role of the Project Manager

If we look at in the widest possible way, a project manager is responsible for:
- Defining the product or service being created, both its features and its specification, and assuring its value to the company.

- Defining the project plan, that is, how the project will be completed.

- Creating the project team, supporting and empowering team members, and leading the team to success.

- Keeping track of everything, catching problems early, and providing course correction when needed to keep on track.

- Managing the delivery process and ensuring customer satisfaction.[9]

When was the last time you defined a team member's role this way in your organization? When was the last time someone defined your role in this way? Many times in ministry roles, team members function as project managers leading others toward a purpose. From Kemp's definition of the project manager's role, it seems that three strong characteristics are included in this role:

1. A project manager defines the goal.
2. A project manager defines the life cycle of the task.
3. A project manager ensures that other team members' roles interface for the common good of the task.

When we examine the biblical account of Exodus Chapter 18, we see that Jethro was helping Moses see himself as a project manager and leader, rather than just a man trying to do everything alone.

Growing in our Roles

Kemp proposes three roles in the world of project management that apply to the world of ministry and Christian business:

1. **From thing- or data-oriented to people-oriented.**

   The key difference is that things and data do what we tell them to do, but people usually do not. We need to relax and enjoy unpredictability and diversity. Once we appreciate the ways people with different skills and different ways of thinking can cooperate on a project, and that the whole becomes more than the sum of its parts, people management becomes enjoyable instead of threatening. (Some positional leaders have others who manage people and tasks for them. This keeps them from having to get involved with people except from the pulpit or the larger speaking arenas. Role diversity encourages interdependence, which necessarily involves risk and rewards of relationships.) Once we get over our allergy to listening, understanding, and sharing, working with people is tremendously gratifying — and it can be lots of fun.

2. **From worker-bee to manager.**

   Like Moses before his talk with Jethro, many of us are used to getting things done by doing them ourselves. We like to be dependable, and we want to be seen as indispensable, but management means less doing and more delegating. It means making a shift from dependable to reliable. A reliable person ensures that things get done, even if they are delegated. Our teams take on projects and deliver results. (Jethro suggested this idea to Moses and the multitudes experienced satisfaction because their needs were met.)

3. **From manager to leader.**

   A manager gets a team to get things done. Project management often requires an even higher level of function, called *leadership*. Some believe that you are either a manager or a leader. Most successful leaders understand that leveraging roles and interdependence to achieve exceptional results requires someone who is both a manager and a leader. Leaders define what needs to be done, or they create an environment where a group can come together and define it. They also provide initial inspiration and develop commitment to a new idea among the stakeholders. Project management requires leadership as well as management skills, especially in the planning phases, in resolving team problems, and in turnarounds for projects in crisis.

Some people have difficulty understanding how roles connect and interplay with the desired common purpose. Geese, however, get this insight at the outset of every migratory journey. I do not know how the lead goose signals the next goose to take over at the front of the V, but in some way, leadership motivates another goose to move to the front. It changes roles for the sake of the flock and the task. Leadership is essential. It certainly takes more than a project succession plan and strong management to get teams working at exceptional levels. Dwight Eisenhower once said, "Leadership is the art of getting somebody else to do something you want done because he wants to do it." [Through observation and experience, leaders learn to get team members to move from the first articulation of the vision to executing the plan. We will talk more about this execution idea when we look at processes.

Other Roles on a Project

Purpose is broken down into tasks. Any organization experiences the ebb and flow of tasks. What is important to note is that projects may be (1) contained within a ministry or department, (2) a project can cross departmental lines and two departments may work together on a task, (3) a task can be so large that it becomes a cross-pollination of many ministry departments or even organization or church-wide. The communication and the exchange of roles across organizational boundaries is important to team synergy. Look at these examples of project organizational plans:

1. **A project within a department.**
When all the workers on a project are in the same department, they report to the same executive, and possibly work on many projects together. A good example would be an advertising campaign. Within the department, people with diverse skills — copywriters, graphic artists, media buyers, and others — work together to design and deliver the marketing campaign. In a church setting, a music ministry is a department with many people working on a large project like an Easter pageant that will have not only church "customers" but also potential new "customers" from the city. Roles within the music ministry team could change and interconnect as the large project moves forward. In this case, the Senior Worship Pastor may become the creative executive while an administrative assistant takes on the role of advertising manager.

2. **A project in one department, with another department as customer.**
In this instance, the work of the project is performed by one group (e.g., the computer systems development group) as a team with a project manager, but they serve another group in the organization (e.g., the accounting

department, in the form of a new computer program that they will use). One department has the project team; the other department is the customer. In a church environment, some departments (e.g., the print media team) provide resources for another department (e.g., brochures for various ministry teams). The relationship of roles between departments is an important connection, and each team's reaction to this interchange of roles and interdependence determines the success or failure of the relationship and the task.

3. **A project that pulls together many people from different areas.**

Sometimes a project is developed under leadership independent of any one department and brings together people and skills from all across the company. For example, when a car company designs a new model, the design team includes experts in customer design, engineering design for performance and safety, and assembly line design for efficient production. That is a cross-functional team. Similarly, if a book distribution company is opening a new warehouse, they might draw people from existing departments in warehouses all over the country and bring them in to the new location to set up the business, train staff, and get systems running. (At the North American Mission Board, we have a cross-function team that enables a large section of diverse teams to connect not only with each other to see what ministries are available, but to go into the field as a unified front. This cross-function approach allows our customers, the staff and lay leaders of thousands of churches, to see a multitude of ministries functioning together. It forces us to share roles and even change roles when we in the field, but if we function well, we are far more effective.)

Why does all of this discussion of roles matter? When running a ministry, a project, a business or a departmental team, we need enough authority, empowerment, and resources to get the job done. Jethro helped Moses accomplish what he had sincerely wanted to accomplish alone, but he was failing. Through shared roles and leveraging the diversity of the people, he achieved not only *acceptable* results, but *exceptional* results. The Bible says that the people left *satisfied*. The people left with their needs met, and the men who used their gifts to help Moses departed empowered and fulfilled. By using good management tactics that utilized diverse roles and celebrated the risk of interdependence, Moses was still able to be the positional leader, yet he multiplied his vision and ministry through the roles of others. The desired outcome or deliverable was satisfied customers!

We can learn much from the geese — and from what the Bible teaches about team roles.

CASE STUDY # 2

A ministry group for which I conducted a team development retreat had some interesting issues concerning their roles. I will list these issues, and then you decide what is best for them.

- They had lost their pastor over a year before, and they were actively searching for a replacement.

- The interim pastor was a team development leader with limited authority over the staff.

- The associate pastor's job description required that he grow the small groups ministry and Sunday School. He wanted to be the pastor, and he sometimes neglected his positional role to "campaign" for the role of pastor.

- The other staff members were diligent workers who were confused in how their roles connected. Their efforts often overlapped, but they also left many administrative gaps.

At their team retreat, we worked through many of these issues, including establishing some Team Operating Principles. There was, however, inadequate "buy in" because of the underlying issues concerning the associate pastor's desire to assume leadership of the church and the interim's limited authority.

Which Goose Leads?

Discussion Questions

1. Considering I Corinthians 12, what help could you offer this team?

2. What challenges do you anticipate when our case study team tackles a large project together?

3. What risks do you find on your team concerning diverse gifts and talents?

MIGRATION

4. What happens when team members do not connect their roles with each other in the midst of a team task?

5. Is there an immediate way that you could apply Jethro's plan (Exodus 18) in your work?

CHAPTER 3

Honking and Hissing: Personal Assessments

The volume of data available on bird migration is staggering. Many universities and animal advocacy groups watch, assess and formulate hypotheses concerning migratory habits. To attempt to discover predictable habit patterns, dangers and flock health, countless observations must be made and tabulated. In this chapter, we will examine the need for good data in our study of teams, including the benefits of providing a baseline, or benchmark, for team development through diagnostics and standardized instruments.

Before we launch into this topic, let me provide an example of the kind of data studied by scientists who observe migratory geese. This day-by-day account is an authentic calendar of bird movements:

Snow Goose Migration Chronology

Snow geese begin their migration in late August. By early September, a few of them appear in Saskatchewan. The big migration across North and South Dakota occurred on Thursday, Friday, and Saturday, October 30 to November 1 in 2003. The following chronology describes the year's migration.

September 7–13, 2003

8th — The first snow geese arrived in small groups in the fields around the Quill Lakes (SK).

9th — Lot of ducks and Canadas are reported around the Quills. A few snows are spotted in North Dakota.

13th — Flock after flock of snow geese are headed south over The Pas, MB area following a heavy north wind. The snow geese numbers in the Quills are on the increase. There are also lots of Canada geese around. Harvests should be completed this week. Additional snows are showing up in ND. Lesser Canadas are coming across the border into North Dakota in good numbers with the last front. Bismarck has its first September high temperature in the 60s.

September 14–20

18th — The number of snow geese around the Quills is growing daily. The specks are thick around Kindersley, SK with a smattering of Ross and snows, however, more and more are showing up everyday. There seems to be quite a few cranes around as well. Duck numbers are up from last season.

19th — A few small flocks of snows are reported in the Des Lacs area.

September 21–27

22nd — Fair numbers of snows are around the Quills and a big migration happened on September 17th. Ducks are thick and Canadas about normal. Hunting success is very good. Lots of juvies are taken.

27th — Goose hunting season opens in North Dakota.

September 28–October 4 (First week of ND season)

28th — There are small, scattered flocks in ND. Six snows are taken by one party in ND during the first weekend of the season.

West central Saskatchewan around Kindersley is real dry. Some good water is located north of there. There are lots of specks with young, and good numbers of Ross and snows with plenty of young. Most of the snows are still north of Kindersley (1-2 hour driving).

October 5–12

5th — Sunday morning (5th), lots of snows were migrating east over Kindersley.

There are unbelievable numbers of snow geese in SK. Not many geese are seen south of Moose Jaw, SK though.

October 13–18

It is very warm in ND and Canada this week.

15th — There are some birds in the Rock Lake and Hurricane Lake areas of ND.

60 snows are reported taken by one party in ND.

Specks peak in western SK. Snows are just arriving in southern Alberta. Birds move into southern SK. There are lots of geese reported in southern SK around Lampman. There are now good numbers of birds in southern Manitoba too.

Migration

October 19–25

The first part of the week continues to be warm.

23rd — 25 mph wind in SK. The weather is starting to turn. Great hunting.

24th — 40 mph NW winds in SK. Estevan gets a trace of snow. At least a trace of precipitation in Estevan during the next 7 days. (Estevan, SK gets 12 inches of snow in November.)

25th — Huntable numbers of snows are coming into the Upper Souris Refuge in ND. One small flock is seen in the western panhandle of Nebraska.

Birds are piling into southern Alberta. They are also starting to come into Sand Lake, SD.

October 26–November 1

26th — It's getting colder. Night time temps in the low 20s in Bismarck.

28th — Birds are packed into southern SK but still lots of birds in north central SK as well. There are a hundred thousand at J. Clark Salyer. A good number of birds are also at Sand Lake in N. SD.

29th — The first snowfall of the year hits ND. There are 2.5 inches of snow in Bismarck, 3 inches in Bottineau, and 4 inches in Estevan, SK. There are 45 mph winds in western MN. A few snows are seen there. There are 8,500 snows at Sand Lake. Some birds are heard in central Nebraska at daybreak — likewise along the Missouri in Iowa. Birds are just starting to enter the Sacramento Valley in California.

30th — Geese are leaving the North Dakota refuges in huge numbers and migrating. The birds have been there in big numbers for only about five days this year!! Some

Minnesota hunters do very well on mallards and bluebills in the Hutchinson area. Late this afternoon, the birds start a major push down the Missouri River and over Pierre, SD. Hunters wait in the Nebraska panhandle for the big push. But, it doesn't happen.

31st — Today, it does happen! The weather of the last two days has really started to move birds. The night time low is –2 in Estevan, SK. The high temperature is 30 and a low of 14 degrees in Bismarck, ND. There is a trace of snow. The birds continue to push through ND in large numbers. They are also moving over western South Dakota. Big flocks have moved into Sand Lake. Minnesota duck hunters are doing very well today and seeing a lot of high flyers heading south in flocks of 200 to 300 ducks.

Farther south, the snow geese vanguard reaches Nebraska by 2 in the afternoon. Hunters report them in the stratosphere today around Omaha. They are going overhead on Halloween afternoon and night near Lincoln and Omaha and northeast KS. The western panhandle has two inches of snow on the ground and the birds are flying over. About 20,000 are reported in one area in Colorado. Dumas, Texas in the panhandle gets 400 snow geese.

Nov. 1st — The low temperature is just 13 and only gets up to 30 for a high in Bismarck today. Another half inch of snow falls. Swans are passing over the Winnipeg area. Northern Minnesota field hunters are having tremendous success on mallards. But, the lakes are freezing fast. Snows are also seen in west central MN. Snows are holding for a while at Sand Lake. Flock after flock of snows are still going over southeast and central NE. There are a few birds flying over central IA. Action is heating up

MIGRATION

at Squaw Creek, MO as northern birds start to arrive. One small flock is reported as far south as Biloxi, MS.

November 2–8

2nd — Not all the birds have left the Dakotas. Snows are on the ground west of Watertown, SD. They are also arriving in Texas and California. Lots of them are around Katy, TX.

3rd — 3.3 inches of snow falls in Bismarck. Temperatures are between 13 and 19 degrees. J. Clark Salyer refuge in ND is frozen. Snow and cold has pushed birds out of west central SK. There are now 300,000 snows reported at Sand Lake, SD, up from 8,500 last week. Pickstown, SD is showing geese in local fields. Small flocks are seen milling around the Missouri River in central MO.

4th — Another 2.1 inches of snow falls in Bismarck, ND. Hunting is just about done in ND. But, despite all the bad weather of the last week, there are still some good numbers along I-94.

5th — Waves and waves of snows arrive in Texas. Rare sightings of snows occur in Utah.

6th — The Sand Lake refuge is emptying out. Those birds form a constant stream of snows flowing over Lake Vermillion, S.D. They are headed for Squaw Creek. Birds are seen in Tennessee.

7th — Tornadoes of snow geese are piling into fields in Oklahoma.

November 9–15

12th — 200,000 snows are holding at Squaw Creek refuge in northwestern MO. Geese are spread out from North Dakota to Texas.

13th — There are still 125,000 snows at Sand Lake. Lots of birds have dropped in at the Lovewell reservoir in KS. The Texas coast is filling up with geese.

14th — Pockets of snows are left in ND two weeks after the big push started. The state is 98% froze up.

November 16–22

18th — There are thousands and thousands of snows in Kentucky.

20th — 300,000 snows are still at Squaw Creek.

21st — Birds are still being taken in Spinks and Edmund counties in SD.

November 23-29

24th — It is reported that there are 350,000 snows at Squaw Creek.

29th — Thousands of geese filled the sky around Squaw Creek on Saturday morning.

November 30–December 6

Snow goose hunting is over in the upper Midwest.[10]

Team Challenges for Geese

As we look at teams and their migratory habits and relational needs, we will examine some other details that expose some of the pressures and challenges geese encounter on their journey. One of the reasons why geese and other birds migrate is to find sources of food. Geese can survive on scarce food while migrating. There are certain glands that produce hormones in a goose's body. If these hormones change, it tells the birds to migrate. The length of daylight affects these hormones. The exact timing of migrations depends not only on daylight, but also on conditions in weather and food supplies.

MIGRATION

In the summer, adult geese molt, losing old flight feathers and growing new feathers. Their new flight feathers grow in time for fall migration. This process presents a challenge because geese cannot fly for three or four weeks during molting. Parents teach the young to fly after new flight feathers have grown, and young geese are taught by adults to take off. Usually they run along the surface of the water or ground for takeoff, and the movement of their wings is very specific. The basic movement of wings contains these components: (1) downstroke, (2) pull forward, (3) lift upward, and then (4) spread again.

Other general challenges of everyday life for migratory birds include feeding habits. Goose bills are very sensitive and are used to "feel around" underwater for food. Tooth-like spikes around the edges of the bills serve as strainers. Geese graze (walk about on a grassy area or a field) or swim and dip under water for water plants, and they spend more than 12 hours a day eating, concentrating their feeding early in the morning and late in the afternoon. What do Canada geese eat? On land, they eat grasses, marsh grass, berries and seeds. In water, they eat pond plants, tubers, roots and algae. In addition, geese feed on crops like clover, alfalfa, wheat, rye, corn, barley, oats and grain left in farmers' fields after the harvest.

Other challenges faced by geese are caused by their wild, and sometimes eccentric, behaviors. Canada Geese have become problems in towns and cities. They inhabit parks and golf courses, eat the grass and leave droppings everywhere. If people get too close to the goslings, the parents may attack.[11]

HONKING AND HISSING

HUMAN TEAM CHALLENGES

Human teams may not face a scarcity of food, but they face similar challenges in other areas. Assessments help teams, organizational coaches and consultants diagnose these challenges so they can be accurately addressed. Every group has embedded physical, emotional and spiritual issues. In fact, humans bring diversity and create risks every time they assemble around a common purpose or task. General Charles Gordon once asked Li Hung Chang, an old Chinese leader, a double question: "What is leadership?" and "How is humanity divided?" He received this cryptic answer: "There are only three kinds of people in the world — those who are immovable, those who are movable, and those who move them!" Diagnostics and assessment instruments assist teams in their discovery of behavioral and structural challenges. These tools identify those who are immovable, those who are movable, and those who move them.

As a coach and consultant by trade, I rely heavily on assessments to create a baseline set of observations, or a benchmark, for team development. An executive pastor once asked me after our initial meeting how I would design their team's path of development. My response was succinct: "Through assessments." He was relieved that it would not be just my opinion and expertise that would design their transformational path to team synergy. Standardized and time-proven instruments would determine the baseline of data as the foundation of a clear, workable, successful strategy.

Humans need each other, but interaction often leads to conflict instead of synergy. A team in extreme conflict fulfills the old adage: "You can't live with 'em, and you can't live without 'em." Diagnostics help determine the behavioral landscape so a clear direction can be identified. That's the only way a team can make progress. They are indispensable in my work with church leaders and their teams. Without an initial benchmark assessment, I feel like I am walking through a behavioral and personality-laden mine field. It is best to know the behavioral terrain before getting too far into the process of team development. In his book, *When the Saints Come Storming In,* Leslie Flynn provides this illustration:

> *"Two porcupines in Northern Canada huddled together to get warm, according to a forest folktale. But their quills pricked each other, so they moved apart. Before long, they were shivering, so they sidled close again. Soon both were being jabbed again. Same story; same ending. They needed each other, but they kept needling each other."*[12]

I'm not recommending particular assessment tools for you to use. Instead, I want you to consider the host of excellent and proven assessment instruments to assist you in team development. The resource section at the end of the book will list some of the instruments in which I have confidence. There are many behavioral assessments, spiritual gifts inventories and team profiles on the market. Beyond these, there are some interesting tools to use for church-wide or congregational diagnoses. In the book, Studying Congregations, William McKinney speaks of the difficulty and necessity of assessing congregations. In his chapter on resources, he writes:

> *"This chapter treats a congregation as a collection of elements drawn out of a wider social and religious*

context that together have the capacity or the potential to accomplish social and religious goals. This frame for understanding congregations has as its focus all the raw materials of congregational life-human, economic and capital, spiritual, and reputational. Resources are sometimes countable (money, people, staff, and buildings), but they are also sometimes soft and relational (shared experiences of coming through difficult times, connections to other institutions, and the strength of members' commitment to the congregation). These soft social resources may be difficult for the outsider to see, but they are no less real than the money in the bank."[13]

Identifying the issues that swirl around in any organization is the first step in providing assistance in leadership development. I recommend *Studying Congregations* because it has some wonderful ways to use diagnostics for groups. It is, however, foolish to focus all of our attention only on that which is easily measurable. All teams, groups, and organizations have layers of behaviors, talents, gifts, skill sets and challenges that come into play at any given moment. The larger the group, the more complicated the group dynamics. However, small groups may have as many challenges and resources as the large ones. McKinney writes in his study,

"Focusing on resources is misleading when we yield to the temptation to pay attention only to that which is easily measurable. Often we hear large, wealthy, or prestigious congregations referred to as 'resource-rich' and small or less prestigious congregations as 'resource-poor.' Such judgments fail to distinguish between resources and capacities. For example, a large

congregation may have more access to money, people, staff, and influence than a small congregation, but it may lack the ability of the smaller congregation to mobilize those resources toward its ends."[14]

Congregational and staff team assessments help to bring goals, visions and purpose into alignment, but social, economic and cultural issues figure into congregational or group diagnoses. Before I administered a tool to measure his team's profile, one pastor told me confidently that his staff team would score high in communication and processes. The results surprised him. Although team purpose was clearly understood, the means to the end was cloudy among his team members. His staff team scored lowest on effective processes and next lowest on clear communication. The importance of this particular assessment, to the pastor and his team, was invaluable. Some leaders are blinded to some of the intricacies of team dynamics, and they cannot see team nuances from their perspectives. Often, leaders cannot see all that is going on in every office and in every department. As we saw in Chapter 2 on roles, the connection points between the roles is important. If the senior leadership assumes communication is great but the team says it is not, what is the next step? In this case, we had to shore up how the team communicated and how much communication was necessary to carry out their purpose. Also, some of the essential team players weren't always in the communication loop, so certain tasks weren't performed with excellence.

This team's weaknesses stemmed from their communication problems. Certain processes were in overdrive, running over folks that were not involved in the decisions.

It was hard for these people to have "buy in" when the process dictated their workdays or their overtime hours but gave them no voice or recourse in decisions that affected them. In addition, there were other flaws in the overall process that caused some missed time-sensitive points in the schedule and accentuated some relational tensions. Without this team profile instrument, we would have proceeded blindly to address a different challenge with a full list of faulty assumptions about this team.

On a grander scale, McKinney's study speaks of another congregational team:

"Melvin Williams provides a powerful example of our distinction between resources and capacities in his anthropological study of Zion, a Black Pentecostal congregation in Pittsburgh. Despite meager resources, he says:

As long as they serve the church physically and financially (often public assistance is a source of their giving), they have a place in the design, a node in the social network. This place gives meaning, expectation and reward to the lives of those whom mainstream ideals seldom penetrate unless reinforced through the Zion subculture.

Williams's study captures several important insights about the ways raw materials brought into the congregation from outside (money, life experiences of members, and social status) become sources of strength for the congregation. In Zion's case, members are poor and struggling. Its measurable resources are very limited. Williams points out, however, that the congregation's culture is sufficiently strong to transform limited resources into considerable capacity."[15]

Migration

McKinney and Williams understand the indisputable importance of diagnostics when prescribing a transformational path for team or congregational health. The study on the Zion congregation revealed that their cultural and socioeconomic struggles were to become their greatest attribute. I do not know exactly what was prescribed for this ministry team, but my prescription would have been to let them rise to their strengths and design a ministry around those strengths. I do not know who said it, but this statement is certainly true: "Things seem to turn out best for those who make the best of the way things turn out." In this case, the congregational assessment led to their transformational path to greater successes. The same was true of the staff team that was mentioned earlier. They were the solution to their own challenges.

Talent Assessments

Coaching other leaders and being coached myself has brought to my attention the value of talent assessments. These assessments may be as simple as a development chart with some key opportunities, objectives and outcomes, or as complex as some of the more clinical tools. While engaged in a coaching workshop, individuals sometimes express a desire for a talent or gifts assessment. When this is administered, it allows the individual to populate their development plan with data that directs them to outcomes that are laser-locked on their talents and gifts sets. Many senior pastors and executive leaders around the country see the value of these tools. In Morgan W. McCall, Jr.'s book, *High Flyers,* the author talks about the value of talent assessments. Examine this edited version of his comments:

"Whereas end-state competencies are a necessary part of the overall picture, a development strategy makes other assumptions. By focusing on ability to learn, it is possible to avoid the trap of assuming that the finite list of competencies important today will be the same in the future.

1. Recruiting and early identification procedures need to include some version of 'ability to learn from experience' in addition to any technical and cognitive requirements.

2. The effective integration of development objectives into the annual assessment of performance is essential.

3. Because development of talent accumulates over a career rather than in discrete annual increments, there needs to be a separate system tailored to this longer-term perspective.[16]

McCall has genuine insight about the value of career assessments for leaders. Teams are made of leaders whose careers are interwoven into a tapestry of synergistic efforts. Surgically assessing, rather than just hoping a generic annual assessment will bring clarity to experiential talent, is best. Before closing out this chapter on assessments, let's make some ministry applications of McCall's research.

1. **Recruiting and early identification procedures need to include some version of 'ability to learn from experience' in addition to any technical and cognitive requirements.** Ministry teams should devise a questionnaire and formal interviews that identify the "ability to learn from experience" factor. Team leaders

should use standardized assessments in the recruiting process; however, the critical information concerning an applicant's innate ability to learn will be reflected in the specific ministry situation and the individual needed to fill a certain position. If you can't find one that fits, it is worth the developmental work to create a specialized assessment for this factor.

2. **The effective integration of development objectives into the annual assessment of performance is essential. This strategy is crucial to all who coach others in their leadership development.** Consider connecting annual, team member assessments to a transformational plan that identifies career development. Sometimes employees grow in areas outside of their job assignments. As more people are developed in multifaceted ways, the corporate pipeline stays full of talent.

3. **Because development of talent accumulates over a career rather than in discrete annual increments, there needs to be a separate system tailored to this longer-term perspective.** It would be wise for ministry teams to consider a separate, annual and quarterly system to develop and assess long-term talent. Coaching is possible in cluster groups with employees traveling together through a development path. Consider working on this system with your team. The collective brilliance of your team members will help identify what should be included in this important assessment tool.

In conclusion, teams are best developed when the journey to effectiveness is not designed arbitrarily. Just as your medical doctor's opinion is only as strong as the clinical tests he runs, the same is true when striving for team health. Assessments can be formal and standardized, or informal interviews. These can bring a clear perspective to team and personal development. Keeping an eye on a team's progress through assessments is a fluid and organic endeavor. Career learning happens while individuals experience corporate culture and organizational climate. The best time to bring some calculated assessment to the work environment is when team members work together.

CASE STUDY #3

One of the large teams that I worked with was eager to discover and correct their weaknesses. People on the team had quite a range of opinions about their weaknesses. On the second trip to work with this team, I saved some time to "flipchart" a fluid discussion on team development needs. One staff member wanted to continue working on general team development. Another saw their personal development as crucial. Several others agreed with the priority of personal growth, but were confused as to the team's overall purpose. The executive leadership felt that everything was going well, except in the area of processes. In a sidebar meeting, the executive pastor asked what I thought they needed to do next. Perplexed by the mixed signal of the fluid meeting, I suggested a team profile assessment. We conducted the assessment, and the results revealed that the team's biggest need was in the area of communication. The lack of communication had manifested some of the problems mentioned by the team, but the weaknesses appeared in different ways to different members. The executive pastor and I agreed to proceed in their team development by working on their communication.

DISCUSSION QUESTIONS

1. Have you experienced the situation of not knowing the direction of your team's development because you didn't have a clear understanding of the actual strengths and weaknesses? Explain.

2. How have assessments helped you in your personal development? Which ones have you used? Which do you plan to use again?

3. Are there any indicators that your team needs a new or more well defined direction? Explain. Which assessment tool might be useful in getting the best data to clarify your team's direction?

4. Are there any long-term career learnings that you believe have gone unnoticed in your profession because of the lack of a specialized system to assess this? Explain.

CHAPTER 4

FOLLOW THE LEADER: LEADERSHIP 101

At first glance, it may seem that migratory birds are just playing "follow the leader." And from a distance, we might think that all flocks are similar in size and species. Around Atlanta and the suburbs, most flocks are small. When they are disturbed, they quickly take flight and land in a nearby field or pond. I sometimes see from eight to ten geese flying in formation over the highways and buildings. They seem to be searching for food, no matter the obstacles or dangers that lurk in urban landscapes. They stay in one place only as long as it takes to feed there, and soon, they fly to another pond or field.

Similarly, some human teams seem to follow a repetitious pattern of ascending quickly to the next project or task only to land a short distance from where they started. The goal was lofty, but the flight came up short of anything long-lasting or world-changing. Some teams, sadly, don't seem to have any goals at all. They appear to be wandering and random in their flight.

Migration

Embedded in the mind and heart of each stakeholder is uniqueness and diversity, and a good management plan will help each person on the team become strategic in fulfilling goals. For geese, their instinctive plan helps them find nesting ground and food. To the uninformed, their actions may appear to be random, but they have a clear plan to guide their actions. This chapter will pursue the topic of leadership, and we will explore the tension between management and leadership in group dynamics.

We can draw parallels between leadership and the migratory habits of geese. Canada geese migrate in flocks that are highly variable in size, depending upon the species, region, and season. Smaller geese tend to migrate in larger flocks, and late season flocks often contain more birds than early season flocks. One scientific report records, "There are seventy-four flocks of interior Canada geese migrating through central Illinois varied in size from 23 to 300 geese and most having an average of 96. An unusually large flock of 1,200 was not included in this figure."[17]

This study goes on to record, "While most migrating Canada geese fan out over northern North America, a few of the northernmost wintering birds remain in their winter grounds and establish permanent residency. Many more move into the northern part of the states to begin nesting in March and April. The great bulk of Canadas, however, continue to more nesting territory, with less competition, and less danger. Nesting in the far north begins in May and June. Smaller subspecies migrate the farthest and live in the northern tundra. Some larger subspecies move only a few hundred miles."

When snow comes to the northern lands, the lakes and rivers freeze over. The geese are unable to swim or find food, so they migrate south to places where it is warmer and where food is available. Migrating birds usually follow the same path every year. These paths are called *routes* or *flyways*. The flyways used by the Canada goose are: the Atlantic flyway (along the east coast of North America), the Mississippi flyway (named after the river), the Central flyway (along the Rocky Mountains) and the Pacific flyway (west of the Rockies). As days get shorter, geese eat more to form a layer of body fat. Migration begins in late August or early September, depending on how far north they are. Flocks travel by day or night. There are at least eleven different species of Canada geese. The species differ in size, length of neck, body shape and voice (type of honk). The smallest is the Cackling Canada Goose, which weighs about 1.4 kg (3 pounds) and is just slightly larger than a Mallard duck. It lives in the Arctic region. The largest is the *Giant Canada Goose,* which weighs about 7 kg (15 pounds).

Migration and Leadership

Leadership traits are both learned and earned. In human behaviors, we find leadership qualities such as:

- Character

- Personality

- Individuality

- Communication skills

- Strategic thinking

- Ego

- Humility

- Maturity
- Passion
- Talent
- Responsibility

When looking at the Bible and how God views leadership, we find that God wants leadership to be practiced and taught, not just learned and shelved. In *Leadership in Christian Ministry,* James E. Means writes, "Spiritual leadership is the development of relationships with the people of a Christian institution or body in such a way that individuals and the group are enabled to formulate and achieve biblically compatible goals that meet real needs. By their ethical influence, spiritual leaders serve to motivate and enable others to achieve what otherwise would never be achieved."[18]

Effective leaders enable others to practice the gifts and calling God has placed on their lives. As a starting point, look at the difference in the synonyms of management and leadership:

- Management — organization, running, administration, supervision
- Leadership — guidance, headship, direction

Another expert on leadership drills further into meaning of these terms and outlines distinct differences:

Management:
1. General: the individual or group of individuals responsible for studying, analyzing, formulating decisions, and initiating appropriate actions for the benefit of an organization

2. Administration: the functions of planning, coordinating, and directing the activities of an organization

Leadership:
1. In a group or organization, the exercise of command and direction in a skillful and responsible fashion

2. Leader: a person who, at a given time and place, by his or her actions modifies, directs, or controls the attitudes and behaviors of others, often referred to as followers.[19]

Leadership and management go together like hand and glove, but a delicate balance must be maintained between the two. When the scale is tipped too far or too long in one way or the other, teams will lack synergy, direction and purpose. Considering the definitions, leaders that over-analyze, take too long to formulate ideas or micro-administrate leave teams in the abyss of indecision and immobility. On the other hand, leaders who do not consider management important often present unclear ideas that are lofty and nebulous visions without a "finish line" and no clear strategy to accomplish the team's purpose.

Let's examine some biblical examples of this blend of leadership and management.

Joshua

Joshua represents the prototypical tribal leader who assumes a new role of military commander. In his story, we can see the balance of management and leadership. In Joshua 1:6, God told Joshua, "Be strong and courageous, for you will distribute the land I swore to their fathers to give them as an inheritance." God encourages Joshua to embody two essential elements of *leadership:* character and confidence. The *management* skills summoned by God from Joshua were for him to distribute the land. In this directive from God, we find the delicate balance in play: Joshua could have just been strong and courageous and never accomplished the purpose of dividing the inheritance through administrative skills, or he could have tried to administrate his job of land distribution without the passion and courage required to complete the job.

Joshua 8:10 tells us, "Joshua started early the next morning and mobilized them. Then he and the elders of Israel led the troops to Ai." In this passage, Joshua exhibits leadership by his discipline to rise early, and he showed his management expertise by mobilizing and empowering delegates to assist him in accomplishing the vision. Obviously, his leadership skills had created a relationship with Israel's leaders and his management skills clarified the strategy.

Isaiah and Jeremiah

In her article, "Contrasts in Prophetic Leadership: Isaiah and Jeremiah," Helen Doohan writes, "Both Isaiah and Jeremiah are affected in their leadership style by the theological convictions emanating from an understanding of covenant. Furthermore, they are professional irritants in the existential situation and respond to changing needs with appropriate reinterpretation of the basic message. Prophetic leaders know their world and are deeply involved in it. However, their religious convictions are the prime factor influencing their approach to leadership and to the world of their day. They give us a politics of faith."[20]

When describing leadership in the context of team development, we have to realize that leadership does not occur in a vacuum: no one leads without others involved. Isaiah and Jeremiah demonstrate leadership qualities that are important for today's leaders. These prophets were inseparably fused to the Word of God, yet they were covenant leaders who had to respond to change. Their convictions benchmarked their approach to leadership even as their world changed around them. Their leadership style rose from their God-given personalities and God-inspired callings. Their *doing* emanated from their *being*. Their management style was based on their covenant, or job description, assigned by God. John J. Westermann writes in his book, *The Leadership Continuum*, "The appropriateness of each leadership approach depends on factors pertaining to the task, situation, and persons involved. One people element the leader has control of is himself. He can change himself."[21]

Leading Through Change

As we see in the examples of Joshua, Isaiah, Jeremiah and many other biblical leaders, leadership is effective when it is appropriate to the particular situation. Teams need effective situational leadership, not sterile academic or positional leadership. Leaders are learners, and only the arrogant refuse to learn. Alexander Pope said, "Some people will never learn anything; for this reason, because they understand everything too soon." If leaders have stopped learning, they cannot lead effectively. As team leaders learn to balance management and leadership, they should always be open to new ideas, new strategies, and new means to become more effective. I have been in some sort of change and adjustment all of my life. Most leaders tell me that change has just arrived, or it is riding in on the next train. (Sometimes it rides hard and quick after the last big leadership conference or revolutionary book!)

Developing Key Attributes for Leading Change

Many aspects of daily change can be delegated, but first, leaders must realize that organizations are organic and fluid. Although the calendar is set and the agenda is firm, things are changing each day. We need to be aware, flexible, and responsive to these changes. Our response determines if they become threats or opportunities. This would include such things as:

- gathering information for analytical decisions

- developing ideas for new methods and techniques

- designing market plans, promotions and image

- developing training and educational materials

- test pilots for staff or task forces to work on

- new paradigms and creative consideration

- new people that enlist and join the organizations

- financial and cultural adjustments

- trends and outside factors

- staff competencies and general human behavior

Some of these items, or at least some aspects of them, can be delegated, such as research and gathering information.

But leadership of change itself cannot be delegated. The leader has to own it. When Jesus wanted to make changes in the Temple, he did not delegate the turning over of the tables! To ensure successful changes in an organization or ministry, leaders must lead the change process with commitment and skill. The commitment to lead ultimately comes from the leadership qualities in the heart of a leader. Managers can become good leaders if they internalize the purpose and communicate with passion. This is an essential and integral part of leading. Joshua acted because he was passionate about God's calling and God's people. Jesus went to His death because His love for us superceded His desire to avoid pain. When leaders are committed to effective and successful change, administrators and managers must summon the attributes necessary to carry out the strategy. Everybody has a strategic role, and everybody must play his part. This is one of the reasons I stay busy assisting teams to hit their marks and their purpose. Leaders often rely on others to carry out change, but leaders must not delegate passion and vision. The threats and opportunities of change require every person on the team to step up, evaluate the needs, internalize the vision, and take bold action. The leader's job is to help each person succeed in this process of change.

Leading through change is a topic important enough for a book in itself. My purpose in this chapter is to present the basics necessary to lead your team effectively in this process. The baseline for leading people through change is the quality of the relationships, not positional power. I'm afraid I have far too many sad examples of leaders who told others to follow without the deep and personal relationships necessary to elicit motivation and courage through the storms of change. The same thing happens with marriages built on positional power rather than sincere love and spiritual foundations. When change comes — from births, deaths, illnesses, temptations, graduations, career promotions or failures — the couple's relationship with God and each other is the only "sea wall" that will last. Derric Johnson hits the mark again in an insight written in his book, *Lists*. He identifies ten **"Paradoxical Commandments of Leadership":**

1. People are illogical, unreasonable and self-centered.

    Love them anyway.

2. If you do good, people will accuse you of selfish ulterior motives.

    Do good anyway.

3. If you are successful, you win false friends and true enemies.

    Succeed anyway.

4. The good you do today will be forgotten tomorrow.

    Do good anyway.

5. Honesty and frankness make you vulnerable.

    Be honest and frank anyway.

6. The biggest men with the biggest ideas can be shot down by the smallest men with the smallest minds.

   Think big anyway.

7. People favor underdogs but follow only top dogs.

   Fight for a few underdogs anyway.

8. What you spend years building may be destroyed overnight.

   Build anyway.

9. People really need help, but may attack you if you do help them.

   Help them anyway.

10. Give the world the best you have and you'll get kicked in the teeth.

    Give the world the best you have anyway.

    If better is possible…then good is not enough.[22]

Our study of migratory geese showed us that certain factors were different for the flocks studied. The flocks of birds were different sizes. Food sources may be plentiful or scarce, and weather affects their habitat along the way. But at some point for all these flocks, a change in the season signaled the impulse to migrate. All of them were taught the similar skills to fly, land, find food and travel long distances. Geese have an innate clock that alerts them that their body fat is changing and it is time to migrate, but each species of bird and each flock has to follow its own migratory scheme. Like these biblical

Migration

leaders and leaders of today, geese must deal with situational changes. As we conclude this section on leading through change, look at the key attributes needed to lead through everyday change:

- Know God intimately.
- Discern His will passionately.
- Pray intently (and often).
- Know that you know what you believe.
- Clearly articulate (at least in your mind) your core values and beliefs.
- Build strong relationships (not alliances).
- Exhibit creativity.
- Practice a team orientation.
- Develop listening skills.
- Expand coaching and mentoring skills.
- Have accountability for yourself and build it in to your team DNA.
- Show appreciativeness.
- Say you are sorry and when you are wrong admit it.
- Look to the future for trends.
- Raise awareness in a broad scope that change is normal.
- Develop a desire in others for change.

- Be a constant learner acquiring new skills.

- Apply the skills to every day leadership.

- Be willing to receive feedback.

- Form new habits that prepare you for potential change.

Which of these are true of you and your leadership? Which areas need some work?

Unlikely Leaders

It has been said that "so and so is a born leader." That statement may be true in a few cases, but it has been proven that leadership is usually a learned trait, not necessarily genetic. One senior pastor told his staff that his greatest aspiration outside preaching the Word and reaching people with the gospel was that he wanted to be a great leader. The statement was profoundly paradoxical. If you *choose* great leadership, then you have to *live* great leadership. If he was one, he wouldn't have to tell them — they would already know it. Jesus blew the top off all former definitions of leadership when He said that the disciples must be "servants" instead of "leaders" jockeying for position and prestige. Jesus was an unlikely leader in His day, and I enjoy discovering unlikely leaders today. Some of the best team leaders I know did not intend to be one. They just stepped up to the plate when it was necessary for someone to lead. Teams desperately need sincere, passionate leaders. Willingness, conviction and a biblical foundation for vision are good starting attributes for emerging leaders. Here are some wonderful descriptions of unlikely leaders:

MIGRATION

- He was labeled unsociable and mentally slow, and he did not begin talking until he was four years old. His own father said that he was not normal and would never amount to anything. He was even expelled from school. This unlikely leader was Albert Einstein.

- This man entered a war as a Captain but was demoted to a Private. When he left the service, he became a farm laborer. This person's progression of rank and career were stuck in reverse and going nowhere. This unlikely leader was Abraham Lincoln.

- This person's childhood music teacher said he had no vocal talent at all. This unlikely leader was Enrico Caruso.

- This man's employers told him that he did not have enough sense to serve customers. He was consigned to stocking shelves and other menial tasks at the dry goods store where he worked at the age 21. This unlikely leader was F. W. Woolworth.

- His editor at the newspaper described him as being "void of creativity" and fired him for lack of good ideas. This unlikely leader was Walt Disney.

- He found himself repeatedly at the bottom of his class, and his teachers said he was too stupid to learn anything. He was finally educated at the knee of his patient mother. This unlikely leader was Thomas A. Edison.

- A letter came from acting school informing her parents that she had no talent and recommended that they use their money for something other than acting school for her. She failed at auditions and struggled to overcome a crippling disease. She could not walk for two years. At age 40, she finally landed her first noteworthy role as an actress. This unlikely leader was Lucille Ball.

Like Moses, Joshua, Isaiah, Jeremiah and Jesus, God uses unlikely leaders to lead teams. Effective leadership requires rock-solid convictions, a commitment to the Word of God and sincere willingness lead toward purpose. One team that wanted help engaged my services. The pre-meeting, which included a development plan, gave me the opportunity to ask some fluid questions about where they were as a team. The answer was, "We don't know if we are really a team at all." After a little more facilitation and strategic questioning, we discovered that the positional leaders were not leading toward a defined purpose. The team was adrift carrying out job assignments, but no one was really leading. It takes leadership to raise a team!

In his book, *Leadership When the Heat is On*, Danny Cox makes these observations:

"The leader endeavors to blaze a trail for others to follow. In doing so, there will be markers along the way. Knowing the organization's future rests in the success of the people on the team, the leader seeks qualities that will lift him or her above the timely into the timeless, thus inviting everyone in the organization to do the same."[23]

Cox then lists 10 qualities that are important to the profile of tomorrow's leaders:

MIGRATION

1. Tomorrow's leader will be organized and know how to establish and work priorities.

2. Tomorrow's leader will establish a never-ceasing pattern of growth.

3. Tomorrow's leader will possess a great understanding of people.

4. Tomorrow's leader will welcome new ideas and fresh perspectives, different from his or her own.

5. Tomorrow's leader will have a keen awareness of team spirit and selfless, organized effort.

6. Tomorrow's leader will be fair and respectful of others, not afraid to question or be questioned, challenge or be challenged.

7. Tomorrow's leader will possess an inner confidence and a thirst for knowledge.

8. Tomorrow's leader will be in shape, physically and mentally.

9. Tomorrow's leader will value creativity and not be afraid to take risks.

10. Tomorrow's leader will be willing to admit mistakes and to change when necessary.[24]

Leadership is that "thing" that surrounds management, structure, culture, organization, systems, history, and people and moves them forward toward purpose. If *calling* lashes us individually to our purpose, mission and destiny, then *leadership* constantly binds teams to their common purpose. Leadership enables a new person in an organization or a guest at the church to see and experience common purpose everywhere they go. The corporate leaders of Chic-fil-A guarantee a consistent food experience with quality food and customer service, and the company franchises their clear, compelling and common purpose throughout the organization. In companies and in churches, leaders must make sure all team members get "it" (purpose, mission, vision or goal) and that their actions reflect "it." In some ways, the Christian world of leadership is different from the workplace. It should be characterized by a higher level of integrity, love and trust, but sadly, at times we all have experienced better treatment in the world than the church.

Look at Derric Johnson's "Ten Commandments of Leadership" found in his little book, *Lists: The Book*:

1. Treat everyone with respect and dignity.

2. Set the example for others to follow.

3. Be an active coach.

4. Maintain the highest standards of honest and integrity.

5. Insist on excellence and hold your people accountable.

6. Build group cohesiveness and pride.

7. Show confidence in your people.

8. Maintain a strong sense of urgency.

9. Be available and visible to your staff.

10. Develop yourself to your highest potential.[25]

SOME FINAL LEADERSHIP PRINCIPLES

A few principles of leadership will work immediately as you start leading your collection of individuals to become a team. Remember, Jesus rewrote the definition of leadership. Look at this passage as we conclude this chapter:

In Matthew 20:25-28, Jesus says, "But Jesus called them over and said, 'You know that the rulers of the Gentiles dominate them, and the men of high position exercise power over them. It must not be like that among you. On the contrary, whoever wants to become great among you must be your servant, and whoever wants to be first among you must be your slave; just as the Son of Man did not come to be served, but to serve, and to give His life-a ransom for many.'"

The problem with Jesus' statement is not our understanding of it. We get the concept. The problem is living it and leading with humility. Just because we can preach about servant-leadership does not mean we are practicing it in our own lives. Kenneth O. Gangel, author of *Team Leadership in Christian Ministry*, outlines this passage for tomorrow's leaders:

- Leadership is servanthood.

- Leadership is stewardship.

- Leadership is shared power.[26]

When I read Ken Gangel's book years ago, my notes in the margin next to this outline expand the outline a little.

1. **Leadership is servanthood.**

    I guess if Jesus wanted us to have several leadership styles to select from, He would have made other statements about them in the New Testament. Although

Jesus sometimes led as a driven and authoritative leader (for example, the Temple table-turning incident), His normal style was living life as a servant leader. Why? He knew it was His nature, and it would be best for us to lead that way.

2. **Leadership is stewardship.**
   Leading is the economy of God's giftedness to us. Will we waste it or use it carefully and cautiously? Also, leading is recognizing that others around us have talents and gifts. Are we good stewards of their hearts and what they have to offer? Have we helped them find their way, and have we enabled them to be all God wants them to be as members of the team? Are we faithful and wise manager/leaders that see the scope of the vision and delegate with the will of God as the catalyst for all of our decisions?

3. **Leadership is shared power.**
   The Bible is full of accounts of shared leadership. God's Word describes many instances of synergy and how teams have greater results than individuals. In Genesis 1:26-27 the Bible says, "Then God said, 'Let Us make man in Our image, according to Our likeness. They will rule the fish of the sea, the birds of the sky, the animals, all the earth, and the creatures that crawl on the earth.' "

   - So God created the man in His own image;

   - He created him in the image of God;

   - He created them male and female.

This passage begins the whole team concept in the Bible. God said, "Let Us make man in Our image." In verse 27, He then describes the "Us" as God. The Triune Godhead is a Team, so to speak, and God is a divine Entity of shared power. Together, the Father, Son and Holy Spirit share leadership, making up the God we serve. Although the Members of the Trinity have distinctly different attributes and assignments, they are the Three in One, God Almighty. We love Them, and we lead others to love Them, the perfect Team, the triune God of Israel! God never intended for dictatorial power to be the leadership style of choice for the church, or He would have prescribed and described it for us that way in His Word. Team leadership is shared power.

CASE STUDY #4

A church in the city has had a long history of success. Unfortunately, the church has declined for over ten years and staff members are leaving at a hurried rate, but the senior pastor considers this to be the natural life cycle of any church. He is a fine person with good intellectual ability. His ideas are good, but he often changes his mind and direction. His style of management is passive in appearance, but actually, it is the same as many authoritarians I have observed. He passively and graciously makes sure he gets things done his way, in his timing, but without truly engaging in very many team decisions. The lay leaders certainly do not know when the next surprising decision is coming or how it was made. The staff does not enjoy team synergy, consensus decisions or the utilization of the team's collective IQ.

Amazingly, this pastor is in denial that the church is declining, in large measure because he is not using a team approach to leverage the lay leadership and the staff leadership.

DISCUSSION QUESTIONS

1. Describe how a flock of geese flies. How does this compare and contrast with the staff in the case study?

2. In your study of God's Word, do you recall other Biblical leaders that balanced management and leadership wisely? Describe them and their actions.

3. Have you ever let your leadership life get out of balance? What did that look like for you and others?

4. In the case study, what are some ways for lay leaders and staff leaders to overcome this problem? Explain.

5. What would you prescribe for this case study pastor to do to begin turning the situation around? List and explain.

6. What are some reasons that leaders of today do not choose the style of servant leader that Jesus demonstrated?

7. What things could you do to become the leader God desires for you to become?

CHAPTER 5

Migration: Process, Scope and Succession

*M*igration is a process. Birds do not convene each year just to honk about going somewhere. They take action. They migrate toward their desired destination where they will find food and safety. In my work as a consultant, I hear a lot of discussions about staff teams planning their visions, missions, purposes and outcomes. For many of them, though, it's mostly just talk. Action requires courage and tenacity — rare qualities in our day.

A few years ago, the Christian leadership landscape was filled with books, conferences and sermons on how to lead. These tools served us well, but the learning was lost after a few months removed from reading the book or attending the event. Especially in Christian leadership circles, workshops have become a crutch rather than the catalyst. In other words, if people attend the workshop, complete the course and get the binder, then they expect to become effective leaders. Of course, that's not so. In recent years, the corporate world has shown that "process coaching" and consulting can provide sustained team development. This chapter, then, will touch on three aspects of team development: process, scope and succession.

Teams do not retain content, even from the best presentations, on the principles of team development without a process to apply the information. I have seen leadership modeled, and seeing it up close made all the difference. Those experiences will always shape my life, but most of the hundreds of books I have read on leadership are gathering dust on my shelves. Let us examine the crucial topic of process.

PROCESS

In a team environment, process may be defined as the "way" we get to the purpose. Far too often, I find teams who struggle to find their purpose, so they "wander in the wilderness" organizationally. Look at some words that define process:

- procedure

- course

- path

- progression scheme

- system

- implementation steps

- method

- route

- plan

- map

MIGRATION

It is a challenge to identify and follow effective processes in the team environment. When one department or ministry is working in their isolated silo, they can pursue their desired outcome with minimal distractions. Process, however, gets challenging when several ministries have to be interdependent. They then need to communicate and coordinate their individual goals, visions and plans with other departments. The overlap of resources, calendar dates, volunteers and finances creates obstacles and pressures. To relieve the pressure and find at least a semblance of success, some teams work diligently to fill their calendars with an abundance of activities. Other teams go on off-sites and retreats to labor over calendar dates, examining the latest and greatest event or program they heard about. We will talk later in this chapter about the impact of settling for good activities, but for now, we will only observe that activities, even good ones, can kill a great organization if they are not surgically placed on the corporate agenda in light of a clear and compelling purpose.

Don't be misled: process is not purpose and purpose is not process. Some people in the leadership world are confused about this fact. Some operate as if their procedures and processes are their purpose, and others carry on their business as if purpose is process. Neither is true, but good and effective processes leverage purpose. Process should not facilitate activities that are not designed to elevate purpose. Process is the strategy by which a team can cooperate and activate resources to bring exceptional results to fulfill the organizational purpose. A clearly identified process defines the boundaries for the team. Without a strong team environment that explores healthy and honest team desires for excellence, process will only facilitate mediocre, bad and ineffective activities. People who are committed to successful and effective processes ask questions like these:

- Why should we finance this?

- Should we really be doing this?

- Does this activity leverage or achieve our purpose?

- Will we get to our desired outcomes by putting our efforts into this idea?

- What are the boundaries and best practices that get us to our common purpose?

- Is this historical event really launching our actual purpose and bringing the desired outcomes in which the organization believes?

- Do those we are hiring, what we are spending and how much energy we are investing at this time really propel our vision?

BOUNDARIES

There are many passages in the Bible in which God draws boundaries to clarify His processes. Only God is omnipotent, omniscient and omnipresent; people have limits. God wants teams to define their boundaries and do the best things to accomplish the purpose He assigns them. Look at these selected verses from Leviticus chapter 34 that illustrate God's idea of process:

The Lord spoke to Moses, "Command the Israelites and say to them: When you enter the land of Canaan, it will be allotted to you as an inheritance with these borders:

MIGRATION

Your southern side will be from the wilderness of Zin along the boundary of Edom.

Your western border will be the coastline of the Mediterranean Sea; this will be your western border.

This will be your northern border: From the Mediterranean Sea draw a line to Mount Hor; from Mount Hor draw a line to the entrance of Hamath, and the border will reach Zedad. Then the border will go to Ziphron and end at Hazar-enan. This will be your northern border.

For your eastern border, draw a line from Hazar-enan to Shepham." (verses 1-3, 6-10)

If the land of Canaan is the land of promise and purpose, then God is demonstrating that His boundaries, whether geographical or spiritual, are necessary for us to function effectively. God's process is strategic and specific. He did not want the Israelites to try to inhabit all the land, but instead, He had a plan and process with clear borders to fulfill His purpose for His people. One of Israel's problems, however, was they were not always satisfied with the boundaries God had given them, so they sometimes wandered off from the effective process and plan and became ineffective. In the same way, most organizations I work with have far too many activities on their calendars. Activities should be designed to raise their vision to new heights, but often, the opposite is true. Their activities have choked out their best practices in exchange for mediocre outcomes. Process boundaries need to be drawn around the explicit purpose of the organization, and the pursuit should go no further. No organization can do everything well. Finances, creativity and human effort need to be targeted for maximum impact. If there are wasted activities, you cannot be the effective organization you desire to be.

God's Process for Gideon

Judges 7 illuminates the effectiveness of God's processes. Here we find the story of Gideon. Look at these selected verses that help us understand effective processes God's way:

Jerubbal (that is, Gideon) and everyone who was with him, got up early and camped beside the spring of Harod. The camp of Midian was north of them, below the hill of Moreh, in the valley. The Lord said to Gideon, "You have too many people for Me to hand the Midianites over to you, or else Israel might brag: 'I did it myself.' Now announce in the presence of the people: 'whoever is fearful and trembling may turn back and leave Mount Gilead.'" So 22,000 of the people turned back, but 10,000 remained.

Then the Lord said to Gideon, "There are still too many people. Take them down to the water, and I will test them for you there. If I say to you, 'This one can go with you, he can go. But if I say about anyone, 'This one cannot go with you,' he cannot go." So he brought the people down to the water, and the Lord said to Gideon, "Separate everyone who laps water with his tongue like a dog. Do the same with everyone who kneels to drink." The number of those who lapped with their hands to their mouth was 300 men, and all the rest of the people knelt to drink water. The Lord said to Gideon, "I will deliver you with the 300 men who lapped and hand the Midianites over to you. But everyone else is to go home." So Gideon sent all the Israelites to their tents, but kept the 300 who took the people's provisions and their trumpets. The camp of Midian was below him in the valley. (verses 1-8)

After God has taught Gideon (and today's leaders) something about effective processes, the story continues:

When Gideon heard the account of the dream and its interpretation, he bowed in worship. He returned to Israel's camp and said, "Get up, for the Lord had handed the Midianite camp over to you." Then he divided the 300 men into three companies and gave each of the men a trumpet in one hand and an empty pitcher with a torch inside it [in the other].

"Watch me," he said, "and do the same. When I come to the outpost of the camp, do as I do. When I and everyone with me blow our trumpets, you are to blow your trumpets all around the camp. Then you will say, 'The sword of the Lord and of Gideon!'"

Gideon and the 100 men who were with him went to the outpost of the camp at the beginning of the middle watch after the sentries had been stationed. They blew their trumpets and broke the pitchers that were in their hands. The three companies blew their trumpets and shattered their pitchers. They held their torches in their left hands, their trumpets in their right hands, and shouted, "The sword of the Lord and of Gideon!" Each Israelite took his position around the camp, and the entire [Midianite] army fled, and cried out as they ran. When Gideon's men blew their 300 trumpets, the Lord set the swords of each man in the army against each other. They fled to Beth-shittah in the direction of Zererah as far as the border of Abel-meholah near Tabbath. Then the men of Israel were called from Naphtali, Asher, and Manasseh, and they pursued the Midianites. (verses 15-23)

Look at several biblical truths about effective processes and leadership from this passage:

1. Gideon, God's leader, got up early and listened to God.

2. Gideon knew where the enemy was located.

3. God showed Gideon that synergistic results would come from fewer leaders not more.

4. God told Gideon to tell everyone who was fearful to go home.

5. God gave Gideon a strategic plan that had scope and succession.

6. Gideon, although not knowing what the results would be, followed the plan exactly.

7. God's technique to discover His leaders taught Gideon and us a lesson: The "doing" reflects the "being" within a leader.

8. Gideon now had 300 passionate and strategic leaders in readiness to begin this process.

9. God now tells Gideon the end-game: you will win with the 300.

10. Gideon took only the items needed to accomplish the desired outcome: (1) pitchers, (2) trumpets and (3) torches.

11. There is no mention of other items that normally are considered for warfare.

12. God's processes strategically omit activities and items that are not needed to accomplish an effective outcome.

13. Gideon had a specific organizational process to win:

    - He divided the 300 into thirds and called them companies.

    - He gave specific instructions and demonstrated how to do carry out the process.

    - He modeled strong leadership by saying, "Do as I do."

    - Gideon fought alongside his companies but led the process.

    - Timing was as important as technique.

    - The plan happened in a certain, non-negotiable succession.

    - By following the continental strategy as lined out by God and Gideon, Israel's leaders enjoyed synergistic results.

    - God's plan was not an additive plan; it leveraged the few strategic leaders to defeat the many.

Synergistic results come from focusing on the details of scope and leveraging talent, giftedness and passions. I do not suggest here that you eliminate your team members or fire volunteers, but the story of Gideon teaches us that teams, when coupled with a process plan and while leveraging the diversity and creativity of carefully selected leaders, can bring results beyond our expectations. Teams are reservoirs of diverse talent, experience and giftedness. Within the corporate brilliance of a team, we find the possibilities of synergistic results.

In the book, *The Performance Factor*, MacMillan says there are two types of team processes:

1. **Implementation Processes** — worship service, outreach event, etc.

2. **Thinking Processes** — planning, decision-making, etc.[27]

Process, then, consist of the team (1) working together and (2) thinking together. In workshops, I express team process as our (1) doing, (2) thinking and (3) being together. If teams are not careful, they will *do* and *be* together but not spend a lot of time *thinking* together.

Thinking together enables a team to find its synergy. Synergistic team meetings enjoy the process of discussions, including healthy divergence as the team explores issues, creativity and interdependence. These teams celebrate the fact that every team member brings gifts, talents and experiences to the table. This is where we find the greatest synergy — and risk — in this type of thinking meeting. Interdependence brings the risk of conflict and high synergy of new ideas which open doors to new opportunities. Pat MacMillan also says that high-performance teams are

"process pathfinders." In other words, rather than continuing to project new activities, events and programming, why not look for better processes to support your best ideas? He shares this easy four-step process to consider:
1. Identify Key Ministry and Task Processes
2. Design and Map the Process
3. Watch the Game Films
4. Implement Constant Process Improvements[28]

For example, don't change Vacation Bible School if it is working well to accomplish its purpose. If this activity is a winner, why not look at the key processes that support it? Fine tune, design and map the processes that under gird it, and then "watch the game films" by evaluating the process, as well as the outcomes. If the activity continues to be a winner, implement constant process improvements. Build in a feedback system that provides you with the information needed to help the team examine and refine the processes. I find that many teams spend hours planning events, but they never examine the processes. They would benefit greatly by working on process improvement.

Done well, process will lead to other victories and surprises along the way. Virgil Hurley writes in *Speaker's Sourcebook*, "A British yachtsman sailed the waters around the Falkland Islands, mapping landing areas, harbor depths, and beach conditions. He hoped to sell a book that vacationers and picnickers could use. In the Falklands War, May 1982, the British used his book and drawings to achieve total surprise when they invaded to reclaim the Islands the Argentines had seized. Had it not been for that book, the British would have not have known about the beach."[29] Clear and effective processes point the team toward their defining purpose and are essential to organizational success. When a team explores issues, recalibrates process and seeks to look to the edge of new possibilities, the journey may reveal surprises of grand proportion.

Process Coaching

Process coaching, through the system of leadership coaching, becomes an intentional relationship of discovery between the consultant coach and the client or organization. Together, they can discover the organization's "best practices." Process coaching should be, by definition, an activity that is fluid, organic and full of life. Process here is more than strict procedure. It is flexible and provides for constant calibration. Process coaching allows procedures to become less rigid than a rigidly structured course of action, and it provides a means for mid-course corrections. Process coaching is more than methodology. It is more like a route that may change on the way to the desired outcome. Process, then, is less like a chess game and more like a rafting adventure! The coach and the client organization make discoveries together, correct things and continue to move through rapid and exciting changes.

Effective process is *the practice of core values* for an organization. It is the living, breathing manifestation of beliefs and core values. High-performance process has more than only one way of being accomplished. It may create change, adjust or abandon the course of action for another that better suits the current team dynamics and path.

Process is also the manner by which an organizational team conducts its business. A process coach shows that strategic mapping is far more than an organizational chart. In other words; process coaching brings out the "alive side" of a mission statement, and the strategic process provides the "in flight" means of getting to the deliverables, metrics and finish line of the organizational core values. As I coach, I often feel like a co-pilot as I assist the pilot guiding the aircraft. He needs constant updates, course corrections and weather forecasts, and that's what I provide for him. God has used me to help a lot of "pilots" in this way. For example, one pastor picked up the phone to call me to get a quick "second opinion" before interviewing a staff candidate. Another, at a coffee shop, wanted to "bounce a few things around" before meeting with his strategic planning team. They did not need someone to tell them what to do, and they did not need to change their overall purpose. They simply wanted to have a confidential coaching session that would enable them to crystallize thinking and finalize their decisions.

Process is also the "how" of the organization, the way that an organizational team deals with team life and team purpose. A carefully crafted process gives boundaries to how the team treats each challenge and obstacle, and a strong and well-defined team process determines how the organization takes advantage of opportunities. A workable process provides a way to sort out everyday personal and organizational issues. Process coaching helps a leader see that decisions are more than top-tier administration. Process decisions involve everybody on the team, up and down the organizational chart. Process connects the "white space" on the organizational chart and fills in any gaps in communication. Each team member, once given understanding of team values, goals, objectives and path, may then navigate individually through a well-designed team process. Process coaching helps leaders enable their teams to live within a strong, values-driven progression that supersedes mere management.

Clearly defined team processes allow each team member within their assigned roles to "see to" the needs within that role. It allows the roles to interplay, but not overlap. Strong process coaching ensures that methods are surgically calibrated, empowering all team members to fulfill the maximum potential of their roles within the greater organization. This enables leaders to leverage the roles of others and to more productively achieve organizational and team purpose.

Coaching, by definition, implies the act of asking, discussing, conferring and dialoguing. Today, coaching does not mean the action of an expert telling an organization how to achieve their core values and objectives, but rather, a process coach listens, confirms and asks about the values, vision and mission of an organization. Then the coach (1) reaffirms, (2) seeks to understand and then (3) sounds out the concepts with the decision-makers of the organization. A viable and useful process coach sees the organization through the eyes of the leaders, but he also has the insights of an outside, professionally trained observer. In its best sense, coaches constantly sound out core values so that the organizational leader will get a real sound and a true reading of what needs to improve the organization's life.

At times, the coach is required to look up historical data or study present organizational data to diagnose the real story. And like a medical doctor, a process coach is interested in the "patient's" perceptions of the organization's health and future. Process coaches should work hard at arriving at a consensus diagnosis of the organizational team's maladies. A process coach refers to empirical research and substantiated findings as he or she turns to the leaders of the organization for honest dialogue. In this way, the team leaders and the process coach make a team decision to pursue a path of organizational development. The coaching interaction builds a bridge to the results, and when this process is most successful, all members of the team cross the bridge to success. Metaphorically speaking, the bridge to team change and increased results is a journey along the path of diagnostic questioning by the process coach and the answers to those questions by the organizational members. One end of the bridge is built upon *present state* indicators and the other side is built on the desire for a *future state*. Getting everybody across is called *process coaching*.

Scope

Scope is another component of effective processes. Look a just a few descriptors that define the scope of a team:
- extent
- range
- capacity
- span
- reach
- scale
- possibility

Migration

We often speak in our staff meetings of "scoping out" an activity, a job, or a project. Many times, however, inexperienced team members define the term incorrectly. The scope of a project is far more than a quick glance. It is a high-level description of what is included and excluded in the project or system, and in the process of completing the project. Defining the scope of any project requires identifying all key stakeholders and getting their input. High-performance teams practice programming and project inclusions and exclusions. Mediocre staff groups, by contrast, seldom debate over whether or not any given activity should be included according to the defining purpose of the organization.

This book's scope, for instance, is to expose leaders to the basics of team development, not to explore every concept in depth. As I have led workshops over the years, it has become apparent that the lives of many people are cluttered with too many ineffective activities. Many teams just "polish up" ineffective activities from the previous year and re-introduce to the church calendar for the New Year. I advocate a different approach: question the validity of *every* program and *every* event. If a team is not making every event or program fight for its life each year, then layers of ineffectiveness will choke out their compelling purpose and clear deliverables. I affectionately call this putting "lipstick on the pig." We take the "pig" of an ineffective activity or project and clean it up without questioning its ability to fulfill its purpose. If we are to put money, effort and talent toward the project, then it must lift purpose and mission.

The discipline of project management helps us define project baselines. In essence, any project or activity has three baselines:

1. The **scope baseline** is the sum of the deliverables. The scope represents all the work that must be done to complete the activity.

2. The **time baseline** is the schedule of all the work that will be done to produce the scope baseline. Each item of work in the schedule is required to produce an *output* that either contributes to the delivery of a deliverable or is an input required by another task in the project.

3. The **cost baseline** is the budget of the project. A budget is the time-phased cost of all the work in the project schedule. The cost baseline does not include the contingency budget or the management reserve.

Another aspect of a process as it relates to the scope of a project is called the "project charter." This is the first document that should exist in the activity or project, and many organizations require this document before the project comes into existence. The project charter *names* the project, activity or event and briefly *describes* it. It *names the owner* of the project, the project *champion* and the *baselines: scope, time* and *cost*. It may also name project *deliverables,* such as internal and external deliverables. The internal deliverables are those that are delivered to the operating parts or components of the project. The external deliverables are those that are delivered to some stakeholder, customer base, congregational group or market. Internal deliverables are the outputs of the project tasks that serve as inputs to other project tasks. The external deliverables serve as inputs to making the stakeholders' deliverables complete.

In addition to the project charter, many large projects include a well defined "scope statement." The scope statement is the defining statement of the project and fits neatly under the project charter. This document defines the parameters of the project, activity or event and is the basis for making decisions about the project. The scope statement is a living document, beginning with the information currently available. As the project progresses, it might be adjusted. For anyone who wants to understand what the team is doing, the scope statement is the chief document used for understanding the nature of the project, activity or event.

Again, the scope of this book is to introduce some basics, not to drill deeply into these management concepts. However, many organizations build a scope matrix that contains project items such as:

1. Scope area — market value, business value, outreach value, change criteria, data, users, support personnel, team members and general public

2. Inclusions — present system, additional operational needs, data and communication, organizational users and outside volunteers, documentation and in-house computers, additional finances other than cost baseline

3. Exclusions —activities and people the project will not support, market that will not be targeted, which data is not needed, volunteers not needed, budgets that need not be used

One last element that is helpful in describing the basics of the scope of a project is called the "context diagram." In the world of ministry, this diagram can be a simple drawing to help the team understand the intended results and the journey to achieve them. A context diagram may be circles and boxes with a few simple lines picturing the project, event or activity. It is simply used to give a visual aid for the scope statement. Make it simple, clear, and easily understood. It shows how the new project, service, event or activity will fit into the organization, department or ministry scope statement. When I work with teams on strategy and futuring, I often use a flipchart or marker board to depict their scope statement. Process is fluid, and it is best served when a context diagram is used to help team members visualize the path or map to their deliverables.

Succession

A clear and comprehensive process contains a succession plan. Succession is best defined by these descriptors:

- series
- sequence
- chain
- string
- progression

Some questions to ask at a team meeting about succession would be:

1. What is the target date for completion?
2. Are there preliminary steps that must be taken before launching the project?

3. Are there prerequisite actions that take place in the succession plan?

4. What are the logical progression steps?

5. Should the team map out an outline of the succession plan before going further to promote it to all of the organization?

6. Has the team played out the chain of events in more than one scenario?

7. How do the segments of the organization that may be carrying out the succession plan report and communicate with each other?

Many teams create a template of events or activities to define the succession plan so that the team has input on most organizational-wide plans. It is difficult for the team to carry out the top-tier management's plan without a clear idea of the scope, process and desired outcome. Team members may become frustrated, disempowered and passive if superiors constantly hand down succession plans without getting their input. Involving the team in consensus planning with open dialogue brings greater buy in and synergy.

Migratory geese follow a carefully designed process to make their long journey. Their process includes scope and succession. A signal warns others that the lead goose is tired and is rotating to the back of the formation for another to take his place — this is process coaching on the fly. Although we will never fully understand this creative masterpiece, migration is a very effective process. Some teams are unlike these geese. They have a clear purpose, but because their process is weak or ineffective, they never truly reach the target, or they reach it late and exhausted.

CASE STUDY #5

So many cases reflect a need to work on team processes that I had a difficult time choosing one. The senior pastor and two other senior staff members led a particular team. To them, the staff were just cogs in their machine. I worked with them on building powerful teams, consensus decision-making, clear roles and action plans, but they chose to do organizational process their old way. In the middle of consulting with them, I made a startling discovery: the lead maintenance man held many of the middle organizational ministry leaders hostage by controlling their room requests and other set up needs.

Here is a real life example of just one process issue that has surfaced while working with this team. The senior pastor and the two other senior staff members bring a vision to the large staff meeting. This meeting includes all ministry staff, who are on the front line doing the daily and weekly programming. The meeting also includes the operational staff, like the head of maintenance and the staff over audio and video, print and web media. The executive pastor shares that they will have a ministry fair involving everyone in the room, and he wants all ministries to begin holding scope meetings with their volunteers. A report to him is due in four weeks defining how their segment of the ministry will conduct the fair. The executive staff member then pronounced, "We need this to be one of the most effective events we have ever had in the life of this church."

Migration

In the following weeks, the children's pastor, who had a large segment of people to attend his scope meeting, promoted his meeting and turned in his set up and room request form. When he arrived early on the Saturday morning to prepare for his meeting that would have around forty volunteers attending, he discovered the room was dark, cold and set up for Bible Study for the next day. He had requested a video projector, seating around tables so they could work on action plans, flipcharts and a large marker board to be placed according to his design on the form. None of these were in the room, and he panicked. He called the executive pastor to see if he could help him with this pending disaster, since these forty people would be there in an hour. The executive pastor was not too happy to get the call, but he said he would find out something and call him right back. When he called the head of maintenance, the executive pastor was told that the forms were not filled out completely. He had been instructed to not consider it a valid request if the form was not correctly filled out, so he ignored the request.

You can imagine what happened next. My next meeting with this team had some interesting dynamics as we worked through this and other scenarios and process issues.

MIGRATION

DISCUSSION QUESTIONS

1. How would you have coached the pastor and his team in this scenario?

2. Can you identify with this situation in any way? (Could you insert one of your real-life scenarios here?)

3. What are some of the process, scope and succession weaknesses you see from this case study? List and describe.

4. Write your own simple outline of a process that would have avoided this organizational nightmare.

5. What do you think some of the relational, behavioral and climate issues that were effected by this process system?

6. How do you see this type of "power play" with the maintenance personnel playing out for other ministry staff members who want to hold scope meetings on weekends or evenings?

7. If volunteers are the corpus workforce of most ministries, how do you think they could have responded to this scenario?

8. How do volunteers view a consistent pattern of process miscues like this? How would you expect them to respond if they don't see positive changes?

CHAPTER 6

FORECAST ISSUES: PREFERRED FUTURING AND STRATEGY

The future will happen whether we like it or not, whether we are prepared for it or not, and whether we help shape it or not. As I have consulted with churches across the country, one of the biggest and most consistent problems I've observed is that many teams are too passive about the future. They have plans and strategies, but they are usually just dusted off from the year before. Leadership requires focused intention. In this chapter, we will examine the need for a vision of the *future*, one that is *preferred* because we have chosen it above all other options available to us. With a vision of a preferred future, we can then develop a powerful *strategy* to see that vision become a reality.

Migrating geese have a built in forecasting system about their future. Their internal wiring signals that it is time to fly. Their brains may be quite simple in comparison to the complexity of human brains, but they know what the seasonal changes are saying to them. In essence, they are forecasting their departure, flight plan and destination according to their natural instinct and creation's

MIGRATION

seasonal signs. Their flight path and implementation steps manifest a strategy. Look at these descriptions of an actual spring migration plan for geese:

- Geese leave at different times; depending how far north they are going.

- The early migrating birds leave in late January or early February.

- Migratory geese fly northward following the melting snowline.

- Geese stop often to feed and build up strength.

- Nesting and egg laying occurs as soon as geese arrive at their nesting grounds.

Geese are remarkable animals with uncanny, perfect timing to migrate either southward or northward depending on the seasonal changes. In the fall, their biological clocks send signals that they should travel to warmer climates and for food. And in the spring, their instincts let them know it is time to head northward to their summer breeding grounds. Let us examine some additional scientific information about geese and their migratory strategy:

- Geese arrive on nesting grounds in early spring.

- Migratory geese may use the same nest every year.

- Geese like to nest where there is a good view.

- They build nests on the ground near water, on small islands or on riverbanks, or in wet grassy areas.

- Nests are built of grasses, twigs, bark, leaves, reeds and mosses and lined with down.

Forecast Issues

- They lay five to seven white eggs, which hatch in about 28 days.
- If geese are nesting in the Arctic, the eggs hatch later, around June.
- The gander, the male goose, guards the nest.
- The female leaves only to eat and take a short swim.
- The goslings are yellow-gray or yellow-brown in color, with dark bills.
- The babies' feathers become gray in about a week.
- Geese can walk and swim right after hatching.
- The goose family leaves the nest soon after young have hatched and heads for the water where it is safer.
- When swimming, the female leads, the goslings are next, the gander follows from behind.
- Predators take a tool on the goslings, and only about half of them survive.
- The geese yearlings leave their parents in spring.
- The young geese find mates and nest when they are about 3 years old.[30]

Preferred Futuring

I've observed many teams wrestling with the future. Ministries, other non-profit organizations, and businesses always are concerned about future things. *Futuring*, or future planning, is not a prophecy of things to come for the organization. It is visionary planning, and the planning process allows us to select the path that promises the most success. For that reason, I call it "preferred futuring." This kind of planning is defined by answering these questions:

1. What is the **potential** of the team or the organization?

2. What is the **outlook** of the organization according to success or failure **indicators?**

3. Are there potential **improvements** within the **desired outcomes?**

4. What are the **expectations** of the organization's **team members** and the **customers** for the future successes?

5. Are there **new opportunities** for growth and improvement for the organization?

6. How would we as a team define a **future state** that had all of our **best practices** revealed in the corporate mission?

7. Are there any **upcoming changes** in the (1) team composition, (2) the economic or demographic makeup or (3) the demographics of the customers that may affect a paradigm shift?

8. Are there **imminent dangers** that could cause the team synergy and accomplishment to dwindle?

9. What upcoming, **known changes** need a well-defined strategy to overcome the loss of organizational momentum?

10. What impending **staff changes** could bring pressures on the team's migration toward successful outcomes?

Many groups have weekly staff meetings that are little more than recitals of problems and repetitions of problem-solving discussions. Without a vision of the future, doubts easily crowd out enthusiasm. Doubtful leaders usually go through three distinct phases when it comes to projects:
- First, they believe it will not work.

- Second, even if they are convinced it can work, they conclude it will cost too much.

- Third, they never thought it was a good idea in the first place.

Many teams spend hours, weeks, months, and even years discussing problems but never developing a preferred futuring strategy. And some teams are great at throwing out ideas and dreaming about the future, but a strategy is more than ideas. High-performance futuring requires the team to clearly frame their future plan. Author Derric Johnson records some amazingly bad predictions in his book, *Lists,* including:
- **"Everything that can be invented has been invented."**

    —U. S. Patent office director urging President McKinley to abolish the office (1899)

- **"I think there is a world market for about five computers."**

    —Thomas J. Watson, IBM (1958)

- "The ordinary horseless carriage is a luxury for the wealthy. It will never come into as common use as the bicycle."

    —Literary Digest (1899)

- "Any general system of conveying passengers at a velocity exceeding 10 miles per hour is extremely improbable."

    —Thomas Tregold, British railroad designer (1835)

- "The population of the earth decreases every day. In another 10 centuries, the earth will be nothing but a desert."

    —Montesquieu, French philosopher (1743)

- "Atomic energy might be as good as our present-day explosives, but it is unlikely to produce anything very much more dangerous."

    —Winston Churchill (1939)

- "I will ignore all ideas for new works and engines of war, the invention of which has reached its limits, and for whose improvement, I see no further possibility."

    —Julius Frontinus, Roman military engineer (1st century A.D.)

- "The phonograph is not of any commercial value."

    —Thomas Edison, (1915)

- "When the Paris Exhibition closes, electric light will close with it, and no more will be heard of it."

  —Erasmus Wilson, Oxford University Professor, (1878)

- "While theoretically and technically television may be feasible, commercially and financially I consider it an impossibility, a development of which we need waste little time dreaming."

  —Lee DeForest, American inventor (1926)

- "I cannot conceive of anything more ridiculous, more absurd and more affrontive to sober judgment than the cry that we are profiting by an acquisition of New Mexico and California."

  —U.S. Senator Daniel Webster (1848)

- "So many centuries after the Creation it is unlikely that anyone could find hitherto unknown lands of any value."

  —A report to King Ferdinand and Queen Isabella of Spain (1486)

As ludicrous (and embarrassing) as some of these predictions seem, some teams stall in the same migratory traffic jam of doubt and the absence of vision for the future. Unproductive thinking and paradigm gridlock cause teams to slip back into lifeless and non-synergistic patterns of behavior. These groups come to weekly staff meetings and do these things:

- List problems
- Prioritize the problems

Then, what happens to team synergy looks like this:
- Motivation and energy decline

- A minority makes the decisions

- Resentment poisons the team

- They experience shortsighted, non-creative and mediocre results

High-performing teams celebrate the group dynamic of *futuring*. These teams creatively look to the edge of possibilities for opportunities and stay postured for a fantastic future organizational state. They ask penetrating, probing questions in their team meetings, such as:
- What will be the condition of this organization or ministry of we keep doing what we are doing just as we are doing it?

- Are there any situations arising that we should address in light of our compelling purpose and desired outcomes?

- What do we need to do — and stop doing — to better position ourselves for the near and distant future?

- Have we checked our team's status to hit our metrics for: (1) the year, (2) the next five years, (3) the next ten years and (4) the long-term future?

- Have we examined demographic, economic and congregational situations that could affect the circumstances of our present team goals?

- Should we shape our team scope and succession plan to better fit our preferred future state?

Forecast Issues

- What should we stop doing that has proven ineffective?

- Of the things we do best as a team, how would we rank them in effectiveness to better posture the organization for the future?

- What would this organization look like "fully grown" ten years from now?

- What action plans would leverage our efforts to claim this desired future state?

Future Thinking and Change

I wanted to include those questions to help you and your team get started in developing your own preferred futuring. One thing we can know for sure is that change is inevitable. How a team deals with change is of utmost importance. Refusing to deal with change is a prescription for team failure. Here are some problems associated with change and future thinking:

1. **Personal issues.**

   Change must always overcome inaction, inertia and apathetic thinking. Without vision and courage, it's easy to stay stuck in the old modes of thinking and the old ways of doing things. Change, however, is threatening. People may become fearful, angry, withdrawn or hostile. This is especially true when change is directly related to restructuring, downsizing and re-assignments in the organization. Some approaches to change management are better than others at predicting personal issues that are common when change is required. Remember, too, that certain behavioral styles weather change better than others. Knowing your team's behavioral landscape will help when you are maneuvering them through change. This holds true for volunteer leaders as well.

2. **Organizational, congregational and ministry team issues.**

    Even when change is not directly related to an organization's structural change, it inevitably results in developing new or replacing old ministry and organizational relationships and habit patterns. Some staff hold these relationships and traditions as absolutely sacred and essential, and they resist change at all costs. Others, though, seem to roll with the changes fairly easily. In non-profit organizations and ministries that are staffed by volunteers, continued employment can't be used as leverage to get people to accept change. Volunteers require additional understanding, time, and heart-felt motivation to help them accept the goals and processes of change. Longevity, loyalty and historical dynamics make ministry change even more challenging. It is important to provide open dialogue, harmonious relations and open and honest discussions. Balancing of all the old and new elements during and after the change is paramount to change success and futuring plans.

3. **Technical issues.**

    In our culture, technological issues can make or break preferred futuring and change management plans. Technology facilitates immediate communication, but if communication technology is limited, misunderstandings and hurt feelings can lead to big problems. The best communication plan in times of organizational flux is simply to have one. Planning how, when and with whom you will communicate your change plan is worth much consideration. The use of technology to facilitate the strategy is worth the team's time and effort. Ask the team these things: (1) what is available in technology, (2) what is best to communicate often (3) how do we communicate accurately, (3) how do we communicate with the right people and (4) how do we most effectively describe the changes. Provide daily updates, live audio and video streaming messages and constant calibration of change scenarios and information for those who need to know. More than anything else, communication builds trust, and trust is vital during times of change in any organization.

All changes have to overcome some resistance from the team, the organization or ministry at large. Some of the major causes for the reluctance of people to endorse change and future thinking include:

- Fear of the unknown

- Traditional thinking — "If something is working, don't change it!"

- Lack of understanding of need for change

- Lack of belief that change will be successful (history of failed attempts to change)

- Conscious oppositions to change based on the knowledge that it can hurt stakeholders

- General indifference

- Lack of clearly defined outcomes

Another result of teams not effectively practicing futuring and change management is a stale team climate and the potential of "scope creep." If a team merely adds additional work to their existing agendas without preparing for change, they can easily feel overwhelmed and lose focus. The scope of their vision and efforts can creep toward ineffectiveness and drift away from synergistic results. This is a root cause for many plateaued or declined churches, businesses and non-profit organizations. Future states always require change, so high-performing teams always experience some forms of resistance. It's inevitable, and in fact, it is a positive sign because it shows that the team doesn't value comfort over excellence. Here are some tips to help overcome resistance:

1. **Inform:** Tell everybody what is going on, what is going to be changed and why it is necessary. Paint a clear picture of the result of the change for every person.

2. **Increase interest:** Explain, diagram and illustrate how the things that will be changed will be better for all involved. Make sure the leadership team gets this message first.

3. **Comfort:** Carefully explain how the changes will not hurt the purpose of the organization, although some people may have to make significant changes. This may not comfort some people who are affected, but it is best to verbalize these thoughts instead of ignoring the issue.

FORECAST ISSUES

4. **Act from the inside first:** Find a few change advocates at all levels of the organization before launching the full scope of the plan on the outside. Team meetings should be the starting place for "buy in" to the anticipated future state, so bring in some of these advocates for team discussions and open meetings before going global with your team's plans.

5. **Provide support:** After finding the constituents who are supportive of the change plan, give them support, information and constant "pictures" of the benefits of the desired future state so they can be effective in representing your vision of the future.

Congregations, staff teams and the public have to be educated to accept change. Charles Kettering said, "We should all be concerned about the future; because we will have to spend the rest of our lives there." In Ed Oakley and Doug Krug's book, *Enlightened Leadership*, the authors talk about the challenges of change and future thinking in the business world:

> *"A 1988 survey of 3,300 senior managers and human resource professionals made this point clear. The survey, reported by Bob Lebow in his Washington CEO magazine article "Making Heroes of the Workers," concluded that of the nearly $48 billion spent on training and change programs that year only 12% to 15% was considered to be money well spent. In other words, 85% to 88% of the time, traditional training and typical approaches to change left business leaders disappointed with the results. This suggests that as much as $40 billion was wasted on training and change programs this year."*[31]

MIGRATION

Sadly, most ministry groups do not spend a penny on managing change, particularly if means bringing in an outside consultant. The cost of ignoring the issue, though, can be far higher than the cost of a consultant — and the costs are not just financial. The hidden cost to the organization, however, may be far greater in lost opportunities, hurt feelings, and strained relationships. What are some of the costs that ministry teams incur if they ignore the realities and risks of change? Here are a few:

- Goals become shallow and shortsighted.

- Enthusiasm diminishes because the vision is less than compelling.

- Disempowered and unenthused team members usually set safe, uncreative goals that can be achieved quickly and without much effort.

- Dishonest and unrealistic assessments of a team's accomplishments bring about poor forecasting.

- The team drifts from their compelling purpose.

- The team re-circulates old plans and activities that have worked in the past, but these do not provide challenge and stretch people on the team.

- Change comes without warning, and teams are caught off guard.

- Individuals on the team stay stuck in a rut, and the customers don't receive the benefits of a fresh, vibrant vision.

Forecast Issues

Overcoming Group Gridlock

Many groups that wish to become synergistic teams are motivated by their desire to overcome stale staff meetings and unproductive agendas. Others are convinced they need to change activities that do not propel the organization closer to its desired outcomes; they feel trapped in an ever-moving, all consuming calendar of endless activities. Why is it so hard to make adjustments? Most groups tell me that they cannot stop long enough to examine each activity, so they just keep plugging ahead doing mediocre things instead of best practices. Business guru Peter Drucker observed, "The best way to predict the future is to create it." Failing to create a future state drains team productivity and saps creativity. The solution is not to focus on surface problems; the solution is to dig deeper into the processes the team uses to craft a vision and strategy.

Examine some of these questions concerning futuring gridlock:

1. Does your ministry or organization most often deal with surface symptoms, such as bad activities and ineffective programming, or does it deal with the real issues like improving process?

2. What message might the laity and/or volunteers be getting in regard to the importance of quality when the staff group continues to fix bad activities instead of fixing the processes that made them bad?

3. Does your ministry staff group focus on eliminating mediocre or unproductive activities, or do you spend more energy increasing the activity load in the church calendar?

4. Rather than working on processes for the future state, does your group settle for maintenance?

5. Does your staff team focus more on what is wrong with the schedule than on what they want to add to the calendar?

6. When your group works together on a project, do they seem to get mired in a problem or do they quickly look for solutions?

7. What could you do more of, better, or differently to get closer to your future desired outcomes?

8. Next year, what will your outcomes look like if you do not change your present activities and plans?

9. What two or three things do you do well as a team that could change your future if you concentrated on them alone for a while?

10. What would your organization look like in five years if the staff and the laity were focused on a desired future state, rather than its present condition?

Use these questions or develop your own. Penetrating questions will surface root issues of vision, process, and strategy to enable your group become a high-performing team. Most of the effort in working toward an improved future is in the shifting of mindsets. The hardest thing to change is the human mind, not the agenda or calendar. Some people do not want to change because it would cause them to have to work harder — or to work at all. These people enjoy coasting. The most they are willing to do is repackage their old ideas. Others aren't lazy;

they're afraid. They feel safe in their present system, and they fear they may not be able to handle new responsibilities, especially if everybody is counting on them. Their minds are consumed with "what ifs." John Stuart Mill, the English economist and philosopher, said, "No great improvements in the lot of mankind are possible until a great change takes place in the fundamental constitution of their modes of thought." Changing people's minds, on the staff group or in the organization at large, will be the hardest —and most essential — task a leader performs.

CHANGE AND FUTURING STRATEGY

I once heard a motivational speaker ask his audience, "Have you noticed that the only people who truly welcome change are wet babies?" A strategy that navigates through preferred futuring and the difficulties of change management must capture the trust of the group members. If an organizational strategy of change leaves the stakeholders behind, it will fail miserably. Leaders need to devise a strategy that enables people to move beyond the natural resistance that comes with change. Oakley and Krug observed:

"The best-performing organizations achieve the highest levels of both organizational results and human satisfaction concurrently. To accomplish this, they must first develop a new framework, or a new paradigm, that emphasizes fundamental yet frequently neglected components of personal and organizational effectiveness. These components include personal empowerment, energy management, quality consciousness, clear purpose, inspiring vision, and alignment. This paradigm requires the development of new approaches that directly

address the real issue: the need to manage the collective mindset or attitude of the people."[32]

One simple strategy for a team facing change can include these tips:

- Focus on what is working, not on what is ineffective.

- Construct a "picture" of what the future should look like for the team.

- List what is working and discuss as a team why it is working.

- Design a strategy based on the tasks and activities that are presently successful.

- Propose strategies that align purpose to goals and action plans.

- Connect things that are working to the compelling purpose of the organization.

- Focus the strategy on the future state, not on problems or existing weaknesses.

- Review the positive traits that allowed for the successes of the organization.

- Plan for implementation steps that lead only toward the desired future state.

- Create a sense of heritage and destiny that lifts the strategy to a higher plane.

- Include a realistic assessment of weaknesses and strengths, and then strategize toward the strengths.

- Calibrate the common purpose for the team and the constituents, and then build a strategy laser-locked on the purpose.

- The strategy structure is the pathway to your desired destination.

Many teams use a strategy matrix and organizational flow charts to depict their path to the desired outcomes. The purpose of these tools is to help the leader and the team think through ways to move from weaknesses and ineffectiveness to a desired future. Future planning and change management are hard work. Just because a team wishes to move into a new paradigm of success and effectiveness does not mean it will magically happen. Teams must work carefully and often on their future strategies. Team meetings then become a tactical environment that eliminates activities that are not effective and adds those that promote a successful future state.

Some leaders use a formal agreement as a part of the team's operating principles in times of change. All team members formalizing and defining a change strategy would concur with this agreement. This agreement would clearly define the change process by promoting similar items, such as these three:

1. Unfreezing old ways of doing things

2. The introduction of new team behaviors

3. Keeping success factors in play in team activities

The team should record a simple, proposed sequence of events that will be needed to bring about the desired future state of the organization. Just the act of eliminating ineffective activities will begin to lift the organization. It is important not to over-think this type of strategy. Simply list what is working, and plan to "sunset" things that are not working. Deciding "how and when" these things happen are the agenda for strategic, high-performance team meetings. Construct a simple timeline that allows stakeholders to be informed, or perhaps actively engaged, in the "sun setting" plan that includes programs and activities. Years ago, a Georgia football commentator had an idea for a simple strategy. He said, "The best way to tackle Hershel Walker is to gang-tackle him from behind…while he's sitting on the bench!" In the same way, the best way to tackle some of our runaway activities and programs is to stop them after their annual evaluations. Do not bring them back to the next year's calendar!

Leading through this type of change is tough at times, but it is worth the effort when you envision an exciting, future organizational state. Often, my team development workshops consist of just two flipcharts and a white board to help us through these things. The team usually leaves the workshop with a document of the desired activities and the ones that they will begin to eliminate. It's just a page off a pad of paper, but it's a powerful beginning. The real work is the execution of the strategy.

Declared and Real Values

Another exercise that works effectively is two simple circles drawn on a flipchart or white board. Bert Ross, our national coordinator for Next Level Leadership Network, used this exercise with a team to help them think clearly about creating a future state and identify action steps toward their desired future. He asked the team to identify

several declared values of the organization. For instance, *declared values* might include:
- We are evangelistic.
- We are mission-minded.
- We are edgy thinkers.

Inside a large circle, we wrote these values. Next to this circle, with some space between them, he drew another circle. In this second circle, we wrote the next set of team values: the *real* values. Most people think hard before speaking this time. Bert asked, "I see what you *say* you value, now what are the real values as *seen by the customer you are serving?*" Eventually, the second circle is populated with statements like:
- We only spend 3% of our time on evangelism.
- We are really behind in our creative curve.
- We talk missions but we only invest 5% of our time and money toward this value.

If you use this exercise, work hard to facilitate open and honest discussion. I usually keep pelting the team with questions until we get to the real values. One team at a workshop started on this exercise in the morning, broke away for a quick lunch and was still working on it late in the afternoon. We scrapped the rest of our agenda because a team cannot go any further strategically than its real values. Working tirelessly around declared values and ineffective activities is wasteful and disempowering for the team and the organization. It may surprise a lot of leaders and teams, but their activities every day may not reflect their real values.

CASE STUDY #6

The team was struggling with identity problems. Several team members had served on the team for fifteen years or more, but several team members had been hired recently to promote their "new" paradigm of becoming a creative and forward-thinking church. The leaders told us they were creative and edgy, and they said they hoped to blaze new trails in church planting and innovative worship. A lot of money had already been allocated toward this new future, but the challenge was this:

- The new hires were energetic young leaders that appeared to be enthusiastic about the future.

- The tenured staff dressed in a shirt and tie. They were kind and thoughtful, but appeared to have many serious questions about the church's plans for the future.

- Just the appearance of the staff connoted a division in paradigms; some open-ended discussions made this clear.

- The deeper challenge was that many people on the team had assumptions about their real values that were not being executed. For example, (using the circle exercise) we discovered:

- What the tenured staff thought was innovative was declared "old school" by the new staff members. (The new staff was correct in their observations.)

- One tenured staff member declared they were evangelistic, yet we could not produce an action that proved this assertion. (Actually, they did not even have a current document of people that had made professions of faith or had been baptized.)

- The senior leadership, dressed in a coat and tie, spoke of how they were innovative. After all, they had started a contemporary worship service to move toward a seeker-friendly paradigm. However, they continued to invite older guest speakers and hold old-time one-day revival services that were not attended by the young seekers of the community.

Unfortunately, this is only the tip of the iceberg of the problems for this staff team. Their declared values were not their real values. There was a definite and noticeable chasm between their *history* and their *future*. Also, the next person they hired was an older, old-school staff member. This addition brought even more stress and tension to this team. No one could really explain the staff hire, other than to say he was an old friend. Hiring him created a deeper division between the declared and real values.

MIGRATION

DISCUSSION QUESTIONS

1. What would you do to help this team? How would help them identify the real problems, not just the surface ones? What processes would you recommend to help them clarify their values and live by them?

2. What are some activities that your team is doing that are not strategic for the future state you desire for the organization?

3. What type of project charter or succession plan does your team use to guide it into the future? If there is none, what could it look like?

4. How does your team practice futuring technique in its team meetings?

MIGRATION

5. If your team is not practicing this technique, how would it look if your team did?

6. Is there a gap between your declared values and your real values as an organization? Explain.

CHAPTER 7

CLIMATE: RELATIONSHIPS AND CORPORATE CITIZENSHIP

*E*very group creates its own climate — an inviting or threatening weather system. The system may produce clear and sunny skies one minute, but moments later, clouds form and storms thunder. As a flock of geese migrates toward their destination, it travels through changes of climate, weather systems and seasons. In the same way, my travels take me from Canada to Florida, from the east coast to the west. I was in Minneapolis last December on a cold winter day, but the same day in Tampa, Florida was warm and sunny. Georgia, where I live, is a transitional winter state. In Atlanta, December often brings a wide range of weather, including snow, sleet, rain and wind or bright, sunny, mild days. The same can be true in organizations. Sometimes the climate is clearly predictable, but sometimes it catches us by surprise. For example:

- A church staff in northern Indiana was in an area where a major company closed its doors. A fourth of the church's members worked for the company, so the staff expected major problems. The pastor had created a high-performance team, however, and they saw this calamity as an opportunity to serve needy families more than ever before. Together, they experienced some tough times financially, but the church grew stronger in every other way.

- A Christian business owner in southern California put a new product on the market. He and his staff expected strong sales and record profits, but another company undercut them. Their sales didn't even cover their development costs, so they were forced to restructure and lay off some employees. The mood of the management team soured more as every day passed, and they blamed each other for the problem. Soon, people hated to even show up for work.

- In a large church in Tennessee, the senior pastor was becoming widely recognized for building a huge facility and flock. Popularity, though, only inflated his ego and made him more demanding. His top staff were quickly getting burned out with all of his demands. The people in the pews were slow to recognize the problem until one of the senior staff had an affair, another became clinically depressed, and another quit the ministry altogether.

- A staff-led church in the rural Midwest didn't have many resources, but they had plenty of heart. They realized that government programs were overlooking many needy people in their community, and they felt led by God to serve these people more than they ever had before. They built a home for unwed mothers, stocked it with food, and found homes for these young moms after the babies were delivered. The leaders and volunteers of this church loved God and each other, and their love spilled over into the lives of needy young women in their world.

In this chapter, we will look at the "climate" we experience on teams: relationships, attitude and behavior that aid or hinder cooperation. We will strive to answer some questions on how these "soft issues" may have tremendous effect on the "hard issues" of an organization. We will examine how, when and why these climatic issues affect purpose, mission, values and vision of any group. Organizations experience a wide range of circumstances, from high-altitude atmospheric conditions to ground temperature issues. When coaching a team, I first look at situations from 30,000 feet, then as we work together to solve team problems, we get down to the ground level to discover the core challenges.

In *The Performance Factor,* Pat MacMillan describes some of the core issues that shape team relationships. He says, "We choose the word solid to define effective team relationships because they must be able to withstand the jolts and turbulence of day-to-day interaction, misunderstandings, dropped balls, disagreements, and bad-hair days."[33] If solid team relationships were a building, then the footings would be the attribute of trust. MacMillan identifies these qualities of solid team relationships:

- Trust
  — of your *character*
  — of your *competence*

- Respect

Migration

- Acceptance
- Understanding
- Courtesy/Sincerity
- Mutual accountability
- Love[34]

All groups face dangers, those that are migrating toward a clearly defined purpose and those who are floundering without purpose. Of course, geese face real physical dangers in their migration, including:

- Exhaustion — too tired from long flight and not enough rest
- Starvation — not enough food available
- Shot by hunters — hunters wait near fields and ponds where flocks of geese land to eat and rest
- Bad weather — strong winds, thick fog, snowstorms
- Flying into things — television and phone towers, power lines, tall buildings[35]

Also, geese have natural enemies that threaten their migratory efforts and cause them to take defensive action to protect themselves. Some of the most common threats include:

- Raccoons, foxes, skunks, weasels, crows and gulls eat geese eggs.
- Goslings are prey for larger birds like eagles and owls.

- Wolves, foxes, coyotes and bald eagles can kill adult geese.
- Hunters shoot geese.

To protect themselves, geese use a variety of defensive measures, including:
- Migratory flocks have "guard geese" to warn the flock of dangers when grazing in fields.
- Geese attack by hissing and flapping their wings, and they may bite.
- They try to chase the enemy away.
- Geese will pretend to have a broken wing to lure enemies away from goslings.
- When possible nests are built on small islands to provide better protection from some enemies.[36]

These threats and defenses parallel the life of teams in churches, businesses and other organizations. Even high-performance teams that have solidified a clear, compelling and common purpose still face dangers while they travel toward their outcomes. I encourage teams to constantly calibrate and recalibrate their activities to make sure they stay on course. When they attend my consulting workshop, team members often find they have to give up pet projects, plans and paradigms. When group members have to eliminate certain activities out of the calendar because they do not fulfill the specifically defined purpose of the organization, there will be conflict and relational issues. You can count on it.

The parallels are obvious as we examine migratory geese and the outside forces that seem to attack them while they are in flight and while they pursue their journey's goals. Look at these comparisons:

Exhaustion

Most of us do not function well when we are mentally, physically or spiritually exhausted. Fatigue causes a host of problems. One of the teams I coached was "corporately exhausted" because of their packed program calendar. The ways they talked to each other in our sessions reflected mental and emotional exhaustion. Climate on teams is determined by their relationships. Like a Doppler radar of local weather on the television screen, team interactions display their current weather system. Team members' behaviors are revealed all along the assessment continuum: personality weaknesses and problems become exposed when people are overworked and mentally drained. Under stress, people usually try to prove, hide, or control. In other words, a team may have driven leaders, passive managers and overly analytical accountants on the same team at the same meeting. When the calendar is too full of less-than-purposeful activities, emotions become raw and edgy. In these situations, don't be surprised if you see the worst in people.

Structural issues also determine the climate of a team. Let's say that a strong staff team has clear goals, strong relationships and high motivation. However, because of "top-down" leadership decisions that are constantly made without team involvement, relationships are hurt structurally and the team's motivation deteriorates. In other words, even though team members have an enormous stake in outcomes and are expected to perform with excellence, they are not allowed to give input to major decisions. A healthy structure would welcome their input and interaction, but an unhealthy structure prevents it, demanding the team "buy in" week after week without the opportunity to give input. This stormy corporate structure will soon cause the team to experience stormy weather— and corporate citizenship disasters as they blame, attack, and hide from each other.

Starvation

Nomadic birds continually face the threat of inadequate food supplies. In the same way, organizational groups may encounter a loss of the emotional, mental, spiritual and corporate sustenance necessary to sustain high-performance teams. What are some of the staples necessary for individual and group accomplishment and team synergy? These are essential:

- Recognition

- Clear roles

- Respect

- Input

- Shared information

- Inclusiveness

- Opportunities for advancement

- Fairness

- Interdependence

- Trust

What is needed for a fully nourished and healthy team?
- Opportunities for creativity
- Shared risk
- Projects and tasks that require team "stretch"
- Cross pollination of organizational assignments (I.e. allow talent from various departments to exchange input and skill sets outside of organizational boxes)
- Celebrate small wins and successes
- Allow entire organization to offer input as often as possible
- Build a culture that includes both transparency and confidentiality
- Humor provides a backdrop to many team meetings
- Family issues and outside interests are allowed to be a part of structure
- Rebuttal is permitted

Team operating principles not only provide boundaries for team meetings and organizational decisions, but they also provide the nourishment needed for a healthy team. These principles are the foundation for good corporate citizenship. For instance, at my first team workshop, a team seemed malnourished. Various indicators surfaced, such as:
- Feelings on edge
- Defending turf

- Lots of interrupting of each other
- Protectionism
- Isolationism
- Rudeness and lack of respect
- Silence on the part of the quieter (and probably the overrun) team members
- Strong egotism and "strong arming" weaker members

These are just a few of the traits I noticed while working with this team in their first step to team synergy. After beginning to clarify their team's purpose and continental strategy, and as we implemented some basic team operating principles, they begin to transform. Their relationships improved over the next several sessions. Even the way they spoke to each other grew more positive as they adhered to operating principles and became more inclusive. A healthy team was being formed. I suspect the nourishment came from the team consuming some of the staples, plus the interdependence they enjoyed in synergistic meetings.

Shot by hunters

Death by shooting is inevitable for some game fowl, and sadly, vocational and emotional death by poor team relationships occurs for some team members. In stormy times of change, the quality of relationships may determine whether stakeholders stay with the team or depart for another. Without stretching this analogy too far, consider the number of co-workers you remember who were lost to the organization because of hurt feelings, a lack of respect or the assassination of their reputations. Many times, well-meaning superiors are not aware how some of their decisions adversely affect people.

After one of my team coaching events, a tenured and talented team member asked to see me privately for a clandestine dinner meeting. He had faithfully served his senior pastor for a decade and a half, and he had taken many a "philosophical and methodological" bullet for his pastor. The senior pastor had proclaimed his appreciation for this man in front of the entire team on several occasions while I was present. Loyalty, it seemed, was not an issue. However, when the executive pastor resigned to lead another organization, this tenured staff member went to the pastor and offered his talents, tenure and experience to become the new executive pastor. The pastor shook his head and said glibly, "That's not going to happen." Although the staff member probably could have presented his case more effectively, this flippant answer crushed his spirit. In essence, he began to die a slow death as a corporate citizen of the team. It was not that he didn't understand purpose. He understood it better than anyone on the team. He had flown the long migratory distances, spent emotional currency, put his own ambitions aside to support this pastor's vision. But when this tenured staff member stepped out of his comfort zone and entered into the dangerous territory of transparent honesty; he was shot down. I tried to comfort him and restore a sense of hope, but he was shattered. He was so wounded, and I might add, so valuable, that he left and became the executive pastor at another church.

CLIMATE

Bad weather

Weather conditions determine the altitude at which geese migrate. From a North Dakota web site about their migratory seasons, we read: "The altitude at which Canada geese migrate depends on weather conditions, the distance between where they depart, and arrive. Under dense low overcasts, geese may migrate only a few hundred feet above the ground. With fair skies a few have been spotted at 8,000 feet."[37]

Organizational migratory teams face bad weather, too. When humans sit in unproductive meetings, work through boring agendas and endure disempowering off-sites, eventually the headwinds of stress and discouragement swirl in. Constantly enduring a lack of respect, the rejection of ideas and petty games played by top leaders create very stormy weather on a team. Volatile climates cause some teams to:

- Fly at low altitudes of creativity and synergy (suffering the loss of out-of-the-box thinking and edgy paradigms)

- Fly above the weather to avoid turbulence (avoiding conflict eliminates interdependence, mutual accountability and healthy divergence which are needed to be on the cutting edge)

- Attempt to travel in subsets or factions to explore new paths to the desired outcome. Of course, when this happens, the collective brilliance and leveraging of synergy is lost.

- Quit flying. Heavy behavioral storms could actually eliminate some team members from the migration all together. The consistently stormy conditions that pummel some teams ultimately cause them to disperse and form new teams that have to begin their journey of team development again.

- Reflect and respond. High-performance teams are very aware of the storms. They respond to the stormy conditions by assessing the reasons and then shift paradigms, change directions, calibrate vision, or become stronger as they fly against the winds to ultimately fair skies.

Flying into things

Unfortunately, migratory birds encounter many man-made objects that can cause harm or even death. These objects may not have been present on the previous year's migration. The birds are caught by surprise, and they pay the price. Cell towers, phone lines and aircraft can stop geese from doing what they do best: fly. Unexpected dangers kill thousands of migratory birds every year.

Organizational groups face similar barriers and challenges. Each unexpected obstacle may cause relational strife and behavioral duress. Too often, the groups do not recover from unanticipated, "outside" dangers. Let me identify some of these external dangers for groups:

- Off-the-chart thinking and strategies that lead to extreme organizational risk

- Confrontation from within or outside the decision-making group

- Financial threats

- Extreme interdependence without clear boundaries
- New paradigms and the anticipation of change
- Demographical and socioeconomic swings
- The drift of purpose, mission and vision
- Unexpected team dynamics caused by new hires
- Sudden moral or ethical challenges
- Unfair promotions or favoritism

Unexpected challenges, in-fighting or power grabs can cause severe relationship problems. Diverse expectations, ethnicity and traditions can cause stakeholders to experience a sense of threat that may or may not be real. In my work with teams, I have seen people react to perceived threats when they encounter diversity in personalities, gifts or traditions. Many groups simply need some good coaching to open up the box, address the issues and resolve misconceptions with honest interactions. Many of the perceived threats are not real at all; they are false expectations that vanish when they are exposed and addressed.

Enemies

All animals have predators. Adversarial competition and territorial issues constantly haunt the animal kingdom. Look at the scientific information that describes the enemies of migratory birds. A Saskatchewan web site on geese tells us:

Canada geese face these dangers...
- eggs are eaten by raccoons, foxes, skunks, weasels, crows, gulls

- goslings are prey for larger birds (eagles, owls)
- wolves, foxes, coyotes and bald eagles can kill adult geese
- hunters shoot geese
- *Aleutian Canada Geese* are listed as *threatened*. Many were killed because of a large population of Arctic foxes and red foxes in their nesting areas in the northern Alaska.[38]

What are some of the enemies of solid team relationships?
- Lack of respect
- Moral and ethical issues
- Poorly defined and implemented vision
- Extreme personality differences
- Lack of trust
- Weak competencies
- Collision of paradigms and traditions
- Authoritarian leadership or positional decision-making
- Unclear roles
- Closed decision-making

These are just a few of the potential enemies that threaten group relationships. Addressing issues like incompetence is often avoided because of the potential of conflict, but team operating principles should include honest and open discussion about employee incompetence. Of course, staff evaluations, assessments and frequent checkpoints help teams eliminate unexpected confrontations. Without operating principles that promote healthy divergence rather than conflict avoidance, groups remain at a low level of harmony and accomplishment.

Protection

Geese have their own ways to protect their flock. Unfortunately, many of the organizations I coach do not have safeguards in place to protect the staff from predictable dangers. Corporate relationships should be protected at all costs. Several protection procedures may be considered a part of a team's operating principles:

1. Clearly written job descriptions

2. Covenant agreements for all employees that include general duties and expectations

3. Enterprise-wide confidentiality

4. Celebration of differences, diversity and departmental assignments and boundaries

5. Operating principles that include disciplinary actions for group controversies and breaches of confidentiality

Alignment issues also bring pressure on any organization. Relationships are adversely affected when team principles do not promote each person's alignment to the team's purpose. As the leader, it is important to lead individual team members toward team alignment. This is sometimes a slow process, and it is probably too much to expect that all stakeholders stay in total alignment at all times and with every team task or vision. David Thiel of Team Resources, Inc. of Atlanta outlines a simple alignment procedure:

An individual team member should be led to move toward alignment of team purpose through these potential steps:

1. Denial

2. Resistance

3. Acceptance

4. Alignment

The relationships and climatic issues of organizational teams often reveal where team members stand in this four-step procedure. If one member is fully aligned and another is in denial, the team is at risk for conflict and strained relationships. If one team member, because of "turfism" or protectionism, resists a newly proposed direction but the majority is in alignment, you can expect sparks to fly. As much as any other factor, team relationships and organizational climate affect the desired outcomes of team purpose.

CASE STUDY #7

This organizational group is dealing with (1) an unproductive calendar, (2) a lot of needless and ineffective activities and (3) relational turmoil. The senior pastor inconsistently includes and then excludes various staff members in decisions and team meetings. Sometimes all staff members and some volunteers are invited to meetings,

CLIMATE

sometimes meetings are canceled at the last minute and only top-tier staff meet with the senior pastor, and sometimes department heads and ministers meet. This team is dysfunctional. For instance, when the top-tier leaders do not want all team members to provide input, they call clandestine meetings that are widely known by all other stakeholders. At other times, the senior leadership encourages honest and open input on everything from new paradigms to toilet paper.

As I talk with staff members about team goals, it's easy to see that the relationships are strained, and the team is losing trust with each other. The inconsistent meeting style is sending mixed signals up and down the organization. Sometimes the concern for the inconsistent behavior of top management is brought out in the open in team meetings, but from what has been evident from team workshops and coaching sessions, many of the team members are very concerned about their relationships and their ability to trust each other. The team is skeptical of decisions that are made from the top down, and team decisions are not fully trusted because they are often changed when top management meets in their private meetings. The larger team is then informed that the decisions previously made were reconsidered by top-tier leaders and have now changed. This team is in trouble!

MIGRATION

DISCUSSION QUESTIONS

1. Does this case study reflect anything that you have experienced? If the answer is yes, describe it.

2. How does it make you feel when you are informed that team decisions have changed after you have been a part of discussions and helped with the previous decision? Explain.

CLIMATE

3. What could happen to solid relationships on a team when this scenario is happening? Describe how that looks in your world.

4. How do team relationships and personal feelings play out in such a scenario? Why?

5. How do relational issues interplay with team trust and corporate decision-making?

6. What kind of actions could be taken to remedy such a scenario?

CHAPTER 8

Honk if You Love Purpose: Team Communication

The honking of geese is a grating sound. We enjoy the beautiful calls of songbirds, but honks are harsh to the human ear. Honking, though, is natural and necessary for a flock of geese. It's the way they communicate to help one another find food, watch out for danger, establish territory, and fly in formation. For our teams, too, good communication is the essential pathway to team synergy and exceptional results.

In this chapter, we will look at several types of communication. The first and most important type of communication is that which happens between individual team members. Secondly, we will consider the communication that occurs between the team and the support staff or volunteers that are implementing the vision. The third type of communication is that which occurs from the leadership team and volunteers to the congregation or organization at large. Many team endeavors succeed because of good communication or fail because of poor communication. Seemingly minor communication problems can block a team's progress and result in confusion, frustration, and failure. In his book, *If I Should Die Before I Live,* Joe LoMusio writes,

> *"A woman who traveled abroad without her husband got to Paris and found this fabulous bracelet she'd been looking for. And so she sent a wire back home saying, 'I have found this beautiful bracelet, one I've been looking for all my life. It only costs $7,500. Do you think I can buy it?' Her husband wired back a short but firm reply, 'No, price too high!' And he signed his name. But in the transmission the comma was left out and the message read, 'No price too high.' Oh, she was thrilled! Omitting the comma almost put that guy in a coma."*[39]

Quite often, an organization's vision isn't blocked by big, glaring communication mistakes; it's the small misfires in the day-to-day communication that gradually eat away at clarity, confidence and competence. Like the proverbial frog in the kettle, people in the organization don't even realize what's happening, but after a while, the team's vision is cooked! A clear communication plan that includes all stakeholders must be established, or it is inevitable that communication will break down somewhere — and often. Clear communication isn't a luxury. It's an essential ingredient of high-performing and effective teams.

I like this story that illustrates miscommunication: A preacher asked a farmer, "Do you belong to the Christian family?"

"No," he replied, "They live two farms down."

"No, no! I mean are you lost?" insisted the preacher.

"No, I've been here thirty years."

"I mean are you ready for Judgment Day?"

"When is it?"

"It could be today or tomorrow," the preacher solemnly informed him.

"Well," the farmer responded, "when you find out for sure when it is, let me know. My wife will probably want to go both days!"

Like this story, some communication gaps are harmless, and even humorous. But misunderstandings and misplaced expectations can slowly poison a team's environment and hinder progress toward goals. Soon, the constituents the team is meant to serve feel abandoned or used, instead of appreciated and served. In this way, the organization's stated purpose is effectively blocked.

Fundamentals of Communication

In order to be effective, a communication plan must be guided by several fundamental principles. These include:

1. Messages should be linked to the strategic purpose.

2. Communication should be realistic and honest.

3. Communication must be proactive rather than reactive.

4. Messages should be repeated consistently through varying channels.

5. Messages should include clear avenues of two-way communication.

6. Communication must be timely and accurate.

7. Important communication should include written and verbal, one-on-one messaging.

MIGRATION

One team I am working with produced a communication plan that guides the team's exchanges on a day-to-day basis. A glaring issue for them is the proliferation of unimportant e-mails. They came like a flood. For years, team members received e-mails from many employees throughout the day, and some lay teams had been given the staff e-mails addresses, too. The result of all of this indiscriminate e-mailing was that team members wasted hours going through e-mails every day. This, of course, prevented them from getting to far more important things. As they devised their team operating principles, one of the first points was a guideline to eliminate excessive e-mails. Their plan focused on making e-mails strategic instead of invasive.

COMMUNICATION PITFALLS

Sometimes poor communication totally blocks a team's effectiveness so their messages never get out to their constituents. The purpose and passion of the team should be internalized by the team itself and conveyed to those they enlist and serve, but in far too many cases, this purpose and passion are diluted before people leave the meeting room. Instead of purpose, team members are confused, and instead of passion, they feel apathy, frustration, or even hostility.

To promote, honest, clear, accurate and timely communication, the team should construct guidelines and principles of effective communication. This is so important that teams may need to set aside their regular agenda to work on a strategy for clear communication. It will be a valuable investment of their time.

Team dynamics affect communication, but times of change pose one of the greatest risks. During periods of change, mistakes in communication are often exposed as symptoms of weak management. Process problems, then, are often products of poor communication. Here are some common pitfalls of communication during times of change:

1. The belief that information should be tightly guarded by upper management and staff at the expense of the entire organization and constituents.

2. Delegating communications to a communications department.

3. Not providing a clear description of the change during the communication process.

4. Not having a strong communication rollout plan and a communication process.

5. Insufficient communication from senior leadership resulting in middle management killing initiatives because they do not think they are a priority.

6. Phasing out or stopping communication throughout the organization after the rollout has begun. (Sustaining the plan is key to communication success.)

7. Failing to identify key stakeholders in the organization.

8. Lack of clarity when objectives are not clearly identified and re-identified throughout the change process.

9. Launching a communication plan without structuring the content of key messages.

10. Beginning a communication plan without identifying which messaging "vehicles" will be used.

11. Launching a change process without some timing constructs in place for communication.

12. Beginning a communication plan without accountability built into the delivery and retrieval of feedback.

13. Starting a communication plan believing that it will not need refinement throughout the process.

14. Failure to consider how to report to all stakeholders after the process is finished.

Although this list seems a bit negative, it is an instructive warning of the pitfalls of poor communication. I've never seen a team that has fallen into *all* of the communication pits, but I've seen a few who scored in double figures! The most important concept to remember is this: building a high-performing team *requires* a strategic and fluid communication plan. This plan must be both organic (focused on people, not just rigid rules) and flexible (able to bend to every situation the team faces). No plan, however, is completely comprehensive and foolproof, but the process of developing a communication plan provides the experiences and tools necessary to solve almost any problem that might arise. Sometimes constituents, stakeholders, and your customers need this plan rolled out in "bite-sized" pieces throughout the change process. This gradual and fluid system of strategic communication reminds me of a story that Michael LeBoeuf wrote in his book, *How to Win Customers and Keep Them for Life:*

> *Tact is one of the lost arts of the twentieth century, isn't it? I heard about a man who lacked tact. He was the type of person who just couldn't say it graciously. He and his wife owned a poodle. They loved this dog. It was the object of their affection. The wife was to take a trip abroad and the first day away she made it to New York. She called home and asked her husband, 'How are things?' He said, 'The dog's dead!' She was devastated.*
>
> *After collecting her thoughts, she asked, 'Why do you do that? Why can't you be more tactful?' he said, 'Well, what do you want me to say? The dog died.' She said, 'Well, you can give it to me in stages. For example, you could say when I call you from New York, "The dog is on the roof." And when I travel to London the next day and call, you could tell me, "Honey, the dog fell off the roof." And when I call you from Paris, you could add, "Honey, the dog had to be taken to the vet. In fact, he's in the hospital, not doing well." And finally, when I call you from Rome, "Honey, brace yourself. Our dog died." I could handle that.'*
>
> *The husband paused and said, 'Oh, I see.' The she asked, 'By the way, how's mother?' And he said, 'She's on the roof.' "*[40]

OLD TESTAMENT TRUTH ABOUT COMMUNICATION

The biblical account of the Tower of Babylon (or Babel) is one of the earliest examples of the importance of communication. In a word study of the original language of this story, we find that the Hebrew word for *confuse* sounds like Babylon. Here is the biblical passage found in Genesis 11:1-9:

> *At one time the whole earth had the same language and vocabulary. As people migrated from the east, they found a valley in the land of Shinar and settled there. They said to each other, "Come, let us make oven-fired bricks." They had brick for stone and asphalt for mortar. And they said, "Come, let us build ourselves a city and a tower with its top in the sky. Let us make a name for ourselves; otherwise, we will be scattered over the face of the whole earth."*
>
> *Then the Lord came down to look over the city and the tower that the men were building. The Lord said, "If, as one people all having the same language, they have begun to do this, then nothing they plan to do will be impossible for them. Come, let Us go down there and confuse their language so that they will not understand one another's speech. So the Lord scattered them from there over the face of the whole earth, and they stopped building the city. Therefore its name is called Babylon, for there the Lord confused the language of the whole earth, and from there the Lord scattered them over the face of the whole earth.*

What do we learn about communication from this passage?

- The Tower of Babel is the building that became a symbol of the builders' God-defying disobedience and pride.[41] Communication is a powerful force for good or evil. In this case, the people of Babel wanted to speak in their own language and stay together so they could defy God Jehovah. Language is powerful!

- The original Tower of Babel was probably constructed prior to B.C. 4000. The arts and engineering had developed to such a degree that they could build a city, and especially a tower "whose top may reach unto heaven."[42] Their knowledge combined with their pride to produce a plan to reach Heaven. This phrase is not mere hyperbole; it is an expression of the pride and rebellion of the Babel builders. The strength of communication, coupled with their lust for power, allowed these people to think they could outshine God. Their purpose, though evil, was fulfilled, at least in some part, by the power of their language and communication.

- The Confusion of Tongues occurred in the fourth generation after the Flood, about the time of the birth of Peleg, which was 101 years after the Flood, and 326 years before the Call of Abraham. At this pivotal moment, God dispersed people throughout the earth, which may account for the variety of gods and the variety of names of pre-Flood persons.[43] To change the pattern of rebellion, even if only temporarily, God interrupted their ability to communicate.

This passage teaches us that clear, compelling and accurate communication is a powerful force. When communication is confused or confounded, it is weak and impotent and fails to accomplish its purpose. When evil factions communicate clearly with their followers, they become a powerfully negative force, but conversely, positive, purpose-driven teams can advance their agendas by clearly communicating their goals, visions and plans.

THE LIGHTER SIDE OF TEAM COMMUNICATION

In Derric Johnson's book, *Lists: The Book,* I discovered some humorous words about words. Let me share a few examples of "Superfluous Verbosity" with you.

- Members of an avian species of identical plumage congregate.

Birds of a feather flock together.

- Surveillance should precede salation.

Look before you leap.

- It is fruitless to become lachrymose over precipitately departed lacteal fluid.

No use crying over spilled milk.

- Freedom from incrustations of grime is contiguous to rectitude.

Cleanliness is next to godliness.

- The temperature of the aqueous content of an unremittingly ogled saucepan does not reach 212 degrees Fahrenheit.

A watched pot never boils.

- All articles that coruscate with resplendence are not truly auriferous.

All that glitters is not gold.

- Eleemosynary deeds have their incipience intramurally.

  Charity begins at home.

- Neophyte's serendipity.

  Beginner's luck.

- The person presenting the ultimate cachinnation possesses thereby the optimal cachinnation.

  He who laughs last, laughs best.

- Abstention from undertakings precludes a potent escalation of a profitable nature.

  Nothing ventured, nothing gained.

- Pulchritude possesses solely cutaneous profundity.

  Beauty is only skin deep.

- The stylus is more potent than the claymore.

  The pen is mightier than the sword.

- Scintillate, scintillate asteroid minific.

  Twinkle, twinkle little star.

- Achieve analysis of your feathered appendages.

  Try your wings.

As ludicrous as these descriptions may be, at times our communication is just as nebulous and confusing. Clear communication is the means by which our team and our followers connect with the vision. From the team's ground-level view, miscommunication is seldom humorous, but from the viewpoint of some leaders on our lay teams, it must appear pretty humorous. If high-performing teams want to clearly convey the message of purpose, vision and mission, they must construct a solid communication strategy.

Before we leave the humor department here a few of my favorite communication quips and quotes from newspapers:

- MAN SURVIVED 17 DAYS ADRIFT ON FLYING FISH

    —Los Angeles Times

- SISTERS REUNITED AFTER 18 YEARS IN CHECK-OUT LINE AT SUPERMARKET

    —The Arkansas Democrat

- CHEF THROWS HIS HEART INTO HELPING FEED THE NEEDY

    —Louisville Courier-Journal

- FRIED CHICKEN COOK IN MICROWAVE WINS TRIP

    —The Oregonian

- BLIND LADY GETS NEW KIDNEY FROM LADY SHE HASN'T SEEN IN YEARS

    —Alabama Journal

- RED TAPE HOLDS UP NEW BRIDGE

    —Milford Citizen

Honk if You Love Purpose

A bulletin misprint emphasizes the need to know the difference between momentum and memento: "Our minister is leaving the church this Sunday. Will you please send in a small donation? The congregation wants to give him a little momentum."

A couple was asked, "What is the secret for staying married for such a long time?"

"That's simple," one of them answered. "One of us talks, and the other one doesn't listen!"

Practical Communication Plans

Most of the content of this book has been developed and refined as I have worked with teams throughout the years. In situation after situation, I've seen the importance of good communication —but it doesn't just happen. It's the product of intention, hard work, and good planning. As I've spent time with many teams, people sometimes have a great idea about communication and "throw it on the table." I often share these ideas with other teams to spur their creativity. In addition, I often give teams some samples of communication plans developed by non-profit organizations. I want to share three of these real-world communication plans with you. Because of their detailed nature, they have been edited, however, the most important attributes of a solid communication plan have been left intact. Use these to help your team find their way when you are rolling out the next big project, program or paradigm.

Communication Plan — Sample #1

The City of Ashland, Oregon recognizes the value of citizen involvement and the wealth of good information and resources that the citizens of Ashland possess. It is important to increase the City's understanding of citizen's concerns, ideas and values so that they can be utilized to make better decisions. The City must identify, create and budget adequate resources to engage citizens and citizen groups to enable them to become a part of the City's decision-making process. Much of the City's overall success is shaped by the quality of its communication efforts; therefore, a proactive approach is needed to foster effective two-way communication. Below is a brief synopsis of their overall communication plan.

Guiding Principles
1. **Open Two-Way Communication** – Ensure that information is shared throughout the community and the organization emphasizing two-way informational flow.

2. **Community Problem-Solving** – Provide citizens with complete, accurate and timely information enabling them to make informed judgments. This will help the City to make the best decisions.

3. **Proactive** – The plan attempts to give the City the opportunity to tell its story rather than rely exclusively on others to interpret the City's actions, issues and decisions.

4. **Decentralized** – Strengthen direct communication between elected officials, City departments and citizens rather than trying to funnel all information through a central point of contact or department. This provides for more knowledgeable discourse, strengthens

accountability and also makes it easier to access or provide information on City activities.

5. **Inclusive** – Including everyone in the process builds teamwork and a feeling of belonging, breaking down feelings of "us vs. them," which are common in many city governments and in many relationships of city government with citizens. The goal is to include everyone who cares to participate and to motivate those who are not currently engaged.

6. **Strong and Consistent Messages** – A successful communication plan is built on strong themes and is more effective than one with unrelated and scattered messages. The communication plan should support, reinforce and reflect the goals of the City government as established by the City Council and City management, thus underscoring the idea of an organization with one common purpose: the citizens.

Author's note: You can insert "Church" where "City" is included and replace "citizens" with "congregation," and you'll find this plan works wonderfully well. I often use this plan in "live" team environments to help teams build their own.

Targeted Audiences

Identifying and prioritizing target audiences are key components of a communication plan. Without these, a communication plan can slip into a "ready-fire-aim" approach rather than a planned "ready-aim-fire" approach. Examine Ashland's analysis of their target audiences:

MIGRATION

1. **Primary Target Audiences**

   A. Citizens of Ashland – Citizens of Ashland are the highest priority targeted audience. Strengthening the relationship between City government and 20,000 residents is the starting point of a sound communication plan.

   B. There are numerous subsets to this audience. Neighborhoods, business clubs and organizations, schools, age groups are all included in this plan.

2. **Members of City Boards, commissions and committees**

   A. While these people are covered under the broad umbrella of #1, the Citizens of Ashland, the work they do on behalf of the community and government makes them a distinct and specific target audience.

3. **City Employees**

   A. People employed by the City of Ashland in its various departments and agencies are an integral part of the success of the communication plan. Each individual reflects the organization in their daily work.

4. **News Media**

   A. The media are important because their coverage of the City Government can have significant influence on the image of government by the public. Media includes a variety of print and broadcast.

5. **Secondary Audiences**

   A. People outside of Ashland, including area resident who primarily work and visit in Ashland.

   B. Other local governments in the Rogue Valley, Oregon, and beyond.

   C. City government associations and organizations.

Goals of the Communication Plan

1. Ensure the mayor and City Council are an active and integral part of the overall City communication Plan.

2. Improve City communication to and from Ashland citizens, businesses and organizations.

3. Improve the two-way communication within the City organization.

4. Enhance and improve community and media relations.

5. Increase awareness, interest and participation of the citizens of Ashland in government goals and activities.

6. Break down feelings of "us vs. them" between the City government and the residents of Ashland, between elected officials, staff and between departments and agencies.

7. Increase awareness, interest and participation of City employees in the goals and activities of the City.

8. Build organizational pride among employees and positive identification with the City government as a whole.

Author's note: You and your team can identify and discuss the correlation between the Ashland City government and your ministry organization. The various integrations of ministry departments, lay leaders and outside customers is paramount in any good communication plan.

Strategies and Actions
1. Strategies

   A. Expand our communication research program, using both quantitative and qualitative research methods to measure attitudes and opinions.

   B. Continue to employ a multi-media and multi-level communication approach and monitor and fine-tune the existing communication tools and seek additional tools. What worked in the past may have outlived its usefulness and needs to be abandoned and replaced with something else. Some people absorb information audibly and others absorb information visually. Be sure that the communication tools are diverse in order to reach various segments of the targeted audiences.

   C. Use interactive communication tools and techniques wherever and whenever possible to involve target audiences in the communication process and increase their commitment to the idea of community problem solving.

2. Actions

    A. **Market Research**

    Develop a list and solicit proposals of market research firms skilled at conducting both attitudinal surveys as well as focus groups. The method of implementation should include a diverse set of tools rather than just one form (random telephone surveys) as in years past. The implementation must reach a broad spectrum of Ashland citizens so that the results accurately reflect the demographic make-up of the community.

    B. **Communication Audit**

    Conduct a communication audit in the next three years. It is useful to review the tools we have in place and our overall communication efforts in order to determine what more we could be doing. Use an outside firm to conduct a communication audit of the City's outreach tools to determine what is missing. Tools may be outdated and tools may need to be added.

    C. **Communication Training**

    Communication counseling and training for city officials and staff is a major ongoing function. This tactic includes communication counseling/training with the Mayor, Council Members, City Administrator and Department heads as well as mid-managers and members of City commissions, committees and boards. We all think we do a good job of communicating, but without the benefit of others telling us their perception of how well we communicate we may never improve. Research firms that specialize in communication training for public entities and arrange for training to be conducted for Ashland officials and staff – possibly in conjunction with the Rogue Valley Public Academy (RSPSA).[44]

COMMUNICATION PLAN — SAMPLE #2

This next sample is much simpler and more concise than the first. As you and your team go through this sample, observe the parallels to your organization. Energy Star provides an instructional site to help organizations to draft a complete communications plan. Look at this sample plan.

Draft a Communications Plan

Using a plan to guide your organization's communications efforts to target its diverse audiences will result in more clear, coordinated, memorable, and effective messaging. Follow the steps below to develop a strategic communications plan.

1. **Determine goal(s)** — You will likely have multiple communication goals, which may include increasing awareness of your organization's energy management program and partnership with Energy Star, educating employees about how they can contribute to these efforts, informing key audiences about energy improvement successes, demonstrating your environmental leadership, and more.

2. **Identify target audiences** — Each goal will have at least one target audience (employees, clients, students, shareholders) and messaging may need to vary accordingly. It is important to identify the target audiences) and envision their perspective and current level of awareness. Knowing your audience will help you to select appropriate messages and how to deliver them.

3. **Finalize key messages** — Key messages are the concepts that you want your audiences to remember from this communication campaign. These messages will be woven through all of the communications materials produced as well as any speeches given.

4. **Determine strategies** — Choose the best strategies to reach target audiences and achieve your goals. These may range from educating all new employees during orientation training to increasing emphasis on energy efficiency and the environment in all materials sent to stakeholders.

5. **Determine activities** — These activities are the actual steps that are to be implemented. If the goal, for instance, is to educate all new employees during orientation training, activities may include:

    A. Adding a fact sheet to the "Welcome Kit" highlighting your organization's energy efficiency successes and environmental commitment.

    B. Developing a 5-minute training video on energy-saving behaviors.

    C. Including talking points about energy Star in the trainer's organizational overview.

6. **Determine evaluation mechanisms** — Each activity should be evaluated to ascertain its effectiveness. There are many ways to determine a communication campaign's success. Information can be gleaned by tracking visits to your Intranet or Internet site, and receiving more compliments (and fewer complaints) on guest cards in hotels, improved staff morale and demonstrated savings on utility bills, and more.

Author's note: These six simple steps will work in any organizational communication plan. A great off-site team activity would be to take use these steps to construct a team communication plan using this sample as a starting place.

COMMUNICATION PLAN — SAMPLE #3

This brief sample comes from a company called Communication Ideas. Again, look at the parallels as they apply to your organization and its communication needs. This company offers a more extensive template for a communication plan, as a paid download.

The Seven Principles of Strategic Communication
1. **Organizational Communication is a management process...**

 ...with a specific business purpose and disciplined methods of development, implementation, and measurements. It is accomplished through a strategic communication plan reviewed and approved by senior management.

2. **Organizational Communication is a change agent.**

   The purpose of communication is not just to convey information, but to change behavior. It changes behavior by persuading people to take action toward the organization's objectives.

3. **The primary responsibility for internal communication lies with all managers and supervisors.**

   The Organizational Communication unit is responsible for designing and delivering the system and tools that enable managers to play their role as communicators. Face to face communication with the immediate manager is the most effective form of communication, and is the way employees prefer to receive key information.

4. **Communication is a two way process.**

   Listening and encouragement of feedback must be as emphasized and practiced as speaking and providing information and directions. Two-way is the only way for communication to actually exist in the organization.

5. **To be understood, communication must be compelling and continuous.**

   While it seeks to achieve the organization's strategic objectives, it cannot do so effectively unless it uses a receiver-focused approach in both content and context.

6. **To be noticed, communication must be compelling and continuous.**

   As it must compete for the receiver's attention, communication must use highly compelling and creative ways to deliver its message. To be remembered and internalized, communication needs to be continuous and consistent. We cannot afford not it communicate.

7. **To be influential, communication must be credible.**

   Without a high degree of credibility, the integrity and believability of the message will be lost, and the whole communication process will be a waste of resources.[45]

These three samples of communication plans will help you construct your own effective plan. I did not include these samples for you to retrofit into your ministry, but to adapt and calibrate to your team's future. Remember that communication is our means to cooperate with the organization's purpose. I met with a team that had incredible motivation and passion toward their mission, but they were failing. When we drilled down into the team dynamics and processes, we discovered that they were becoming immobilized by an undefined and ineffective communication plan. In their case, every person on the team had their own instinctive style, but differing expectations led to big problems. One department did not know the other departments' plans and implementation steps, and the congregation did not have a clear picture of the steps to the mission. The strong lay leadership base struggled to understand exactly when, where and how the mission was to be accomplished. Their motives were pure and they exhibited enormous energy, but the plan was being drained all of the synergy by poor communication. A team can go no further than strong, clear, accurate, timely and urgent communication can facilitate. Don't make assumptions about communications on your team. Talk about it, wrestle with it, and develop a plan that works for your team.

CASE STUDY #8

A very energetic church team asked me to work with them on high-performance decision-making. This particular workshop normally takes one day, but we decided to work the second day on real programming and event issues. The team grasped the decision-making concepts without a problem, but when we got down to strategic thinking and planning, they hit a major roadblock. Without revealing too much of their situation, let me describe the impasse:

- Their purpose was clear, and the staff was enthusiastic, but they were missing their projections.

- Highly skilled and tenured staff members were leading each major department or ministry team.

- When I wrote their (1) purpose, (2) their inputs, (3) their activities and (4) their outcomes on a flipchart, a significant issue surfaced: they were trying to maintain 210 activities on their church calendar.

- In their enthusiasm, they had not put into place a communication plan that "cross-pollinated" the organization to keep some activities from ever getting to the permanent agenda. In other words, every agenda item was accepted, then it was financed and propelled by money, volunteer or leadership effort.

- Ultimately, the quality and quantity of the team's communication was dwindling because they were busy trying to keep up with too many good things. Their "best practices" could not happen because their communication plan did not provide for them.

- If an idea seemed good to one department, it was then placed on the calendar and financed. The team as a whole had no way of ever providing enough dialogue to stop some of these things. The result was an accumulation of layers of good things rather than a few best things that could lift the compelling purpose of the team and organization.

Discussion Questions

1. After a couple of years of working in this environment, what do think might be the stress levels of the staff? How do you think they related to each other?

2. How would you construct a communication plan to assist this team scenario? What elements would you include? Explain.

3. What are some common communication pitfalls in your working environment?

4. How would you propose to begin to eliminate these pitfalls?

MIGRATION

5. What programs or activities demand an individual, specific communication plan because of their enormity? Explain.

6. How do you see that communication is the means by which those we lead may cooperate with the team's vision?

CHAPTER 9

Cyclical Migration: Continuation and Team Building

The rhythms of geese migration are as predictable as the seasons. For countless generations, they have gathered together in the spring to fly north to breed, and when the chill of fall is in the air, they fly south to find food for themselves and their new offspring. Cycles are seen throughout nature: seasons; day and night; birth, youth, productive years, old age and death. Solomon observed this pattern very clearly. In Ecclesiastes, he wrote:

> *A generation goes and a generation comes, but the earth remains forever. The sun rises and the sun sets; panting, [it returns] to its place where it rises. Gusting to the south, turning to the north, turning, turning goes the wind, and the wind returns its cycles. All the streams flow to the sea, yet the sea is never full. The streams are flowing to the place, and they flow there again. All things are wearisome; man is unable to speak. The eye is not satisfied by seeing or the ear filled with hearing. What has been is what will be, and what has been done is what will be done; there is nothing new under the sun. (Ecc. 1:4-9)*

MIGRATION

Cycles are normal and predictable. The word "cycle" includes definitions that are a good starting point for this chapter. The word means "a series." The process of team development is a series of events. Teams do not become dynamic and synergistic overnight, and they do not become high performing simply because people attend a workshop. Teams, like families, experience life in a series of events. Some of these happen daily, some weekly and some over long periods.

Cycles are also "sequential." Each step follows another in a predictable pattern. In fact, our lives would be utter chaos if life were not fairly predictable. The sequence of team development is, as we have seen, intentional. Good planning, or futuring, keeps the team on track so that the sequence produces positive results. But I've also seen teams endure the negative sequence of a weak vision, which produces poor planning, discouragement, blaming and hiding, and finally, disintegration. In these cases, the seasons of change come rushing in, almost as an intruder, to bring stress, pain and pressures to the team. A sequence is natural and predictable, and it can be guided by the principles of team development.

As I've worked with many teams over the years, I've noticed *outside influences* on their experience of cycles. Sometimes, positive circumstances (such as an addition of a great team player, heightened levels of communication at a workshop, or a new, bold vision that captures the team's imagination) build team synergy. But negative influences (such as an arbitrary and harmful decision by a manager above the team, or a tragedy that affects families of team members) can destroy the team's climate and culture. More often, however, I've seen *internal influences* shape teams for good or ill. Poor choices by the entire team or individuals on the team can erode or shatter trust. Good communication, though, builds trust even in the toughest of times. Some teams, in fact, grow closer and stronger during times of stress and tragedy because they learn they can depend on each other. Highly developed teams become observant and often can predict the impact of positive and negative influences. They can then capitalize on the positive influences —internal or external ones — and minimize the damage of the negative ones.

Team cycles can also be described as "phases." For instance, one team may be further along in their team development than another team. Or in an organization like a church, the staff team could be fine-tuning their effectiveness because they've already developed a significant measure of trust, while the lay volunteer teams are just beginning to trust each other. The observation of phases on teams is not an exact science, but various teams can be at different phases of development for a variety of reasons. Look at a few reasons how and why this happens:

- Sometimes it is good to select a "champion" or "model" team in a large organization as a "proof of concept" prototype. In this case, the "roll out" team will lead the organization in team development.

- Some teams prove to be resistant to the principles and practices of team development, and their progress is stunted. In this case, another team may begin developing and quickly surpass the original team.

- Some staff teams are resistant to change, but teams of lay volunteers may be far more willing to embrace the team concepts and move ahead of the staff.

- Tremendous effort and attention are required for a change to become a new norm in an organization. If the initial efforts are not continued, the team probably will revert back to previous patterns of thought and behavior. They will then have to restart the team development cycle to make progress again.

- When senior leadership changes, adjustments are invariably necessary for the team members.

Continuation

Team development is difficult to sustain without adequate coaching. Process coaching and consulting enable teams to stay healthy and on a course for high performance. A team continuance plan may include periodic assessments, off-sites for reviewing metrics and written covenants. My executive coach provides affirmations and corrections in an effective continuance plan for me. He asks strategic questions, and carefully and intentionally keeps me on the path of personal development. For synergistic and sustained improvement, your team needs someone to provide this vital assistance. A coach or consultant helps you and your team continue to move forward.

In my consulting with church staff, I've seen many associate pastors or executive pastors keep a watchful eye on their team's development. I call them my "project champions." These champions, along with their leadership coach, calibrate and tune their team members into the concepts experienced in the workshops or team sessions. Quite often, teams experience unexpected roadblocks or resistance from someone on the team. In these cases, the coach can address the problem and keep them on track.

CYCLICAL MIGRATION

Sometimes a team's continuation is defined only by maintenance, not progress. This is not the most positive scenario, but it is a lot better than a downward spiral of team disintegration. Occasionally, teams that initially showed promise stop, slip backward and become stale, disjointed collections of individuals again. Some even become fighting factions and warring mobs! Positive or negative movement depends on the seasons of change and outside forces that influence the team's climate. A change of leadership, conflicting paradigms, economic factors or moral and ethical failures can shake up a team. In these stressful times, maintenance could be a worthy goal, the stopgap against further decline. Even when maintenance instead of progress is the goal, continuance requires careful guidance.

Teams grow by continuing —week after week and year after year — to practice positive team dynamics and concepts. Keeping a team moving forward is important. I suggest that teams keep working together, practicing their team operating principles and enjoy synergistic meetings. I try to help them move toward their preferred future and practice the fundamentals of sound team development along the journey.

If you are the team champion or if you are an aspiring coach, use some of these strategic questions to get a slipping team back on track:

- **What are the basics of good team health?** Have people list these characteristics in a team meeting. Allow time for hearty discussion and flipchart the team's discussions. This exercise keeps the group considering continuance and a logical sequence of team development and health.

- **What are the essentials that must be carried forward in team development?** Have the team members sort out which team activities should stay and which should go away. Again, have them dialogue about the essentials and capture their observations on a flipchart. Sometimes I ask, "If we could only do *one or two things* well together as a staff team, what would those essentials be?" In a "live" team meeting, list these and revisit from time to time. This helps to keep process and team development a living and organic occurrence, rather than just an activity at a team retreat.

- **What are the *good practices* that we could lay aside to make room for the *best practices*?** This is not just a time-consuming exercise to soak up team meeting time. Continuance and on-going team development are as intentional as nutrition and exercise. If you wait until the annual retreat to practice these things, it's like running six miles once a year for exercise: it's painful and unproductive! Find ways to separate the good from the best in frequent discussions with the team.

- **What should we stop doing as a team and as an organization?** This question is guaranteed to create energetic team discussions! This activity, if practiced often, will eliminate the accumulation of ineffective activities and unfocused paradigms.

The processes of developing as a team can be as exciting as the destinations and outcomes themselves. As the leader of my family, most of the things I remember about vacation are not the actual destinations, but the automobile rides and the funny experiences along the way. Do not neglect to value the team's journey. If you and your team pay attention along the way, you'll uncover some unbelievable ideas and discover wonderful personal stories. The team will grow stronger, and you'll enjoy the path to the fulfillment of your team's mission. Make the team's continuation plan exciting and fluid for your team members.

TEAM TIME

Since teams are individuals moving together toward a desired outcome and mission, time is always an important factor. Deadlines can be fierce taskmasters, but it is imperative that teams find time to make course corrections. In my work with teams, we often employ an activity that uses a carpet that gives off electronic signals. In this exercise, people know the clock is running, so they pick up their pace. In fact, many teams jump right into the activity without planning their strategy. That's natural, but it's counterproductive. Teams need to realize that the clock is running, but they need to *stop doing* long enough to *start thinking* together. As teams continue along this path of team development, they must carve out time to pull aside, think, and pray about what is going on. Let's look again at Solomon's insights in Ecclesiastes:

There is an occasion for everything, and a time for
every activity under heaven:
A time to give birth and a time to die;
A time to plant and a time to uproot;
A time to kill and a time to heal;
A time to tear down and a time to build;
A time to weep and a time to laugh;

A time to mourn and a time to dance;
A time to throw stones and a time to gather stones;
A time to embrace and a time to avoid embracing;
A time to search and a time to count as lost;
A time to keep and a time to throw away;
A time to tear and a time to sew;
A time to be silent and a time to speak;
A time to love and a time to hate;
A time for war and a time for peace. (Ecc. 3: 1-8)

This passage contains a few things that modern day teams do not experience, but it is a remarkable how the passage speaks of many events common to today's teams. High-performance teams deal with these continuation processes effectively. Some parallels from this passage include:

- Organizations birth new ideas and old ones die. There is a time for both to happen.

- Organizations plant and water goals and visions and learn to uproot ineffective ones.

- Organizations tear down buildings and old paradigms, and they build back according to their purpose.

- Organizations embrace new concepts, and they practice not embracing everything that comes down the pike.

- Organizations should sometimes speak out on issues, and sometimes they should remain silent.

- Organizations sometimes must stand up and fight for what is right, but at other times, they should be peacemakers.

CYCLICAL MIGRATION

Sustaining team synergy requires the continuous practice of sorting through what is relevant and irrelevant. As I mentioned in the strategic questioning exercises, team development is the unremitting action of separating what is *good* from what is *best*. I've noticed that teams on the move toward a high-performing future have a continuation plan in place; those without a plan often are mired in mediocrity. Whether the team develops its own continuation plan or engages a coach, this plan is essential.

There are many teambuilding activities, games and templates for action plans. In the appendix, I have included contact information to help you find some tools that will work for you. In addition, the resources section includes companies that sell teambuilding materials. Our organization, Next Level Leadership Network, conducts workshops that deal with teambuilding, communication, conflict, meetings and decision-making. We promote process consulting, coaching and strategy events to assist teams in their development. Here are a few ways that leadership coaches assist teams with their continuous development:

- Off-sites

- Retreats

- Team assessments

- Executive coaching

- White board and flipchart sessions

- Strategy and futuring workshops

- Research, articles and web support

Migration

Process Coaching

I want to remind you of a couple of key concepts that assist teams in the continuation process:

- Every individual that wishes to grow in leadership development needs to consider a process or "life" coach.

- Most teams must have a process coach to connect the concepts needed in team development.

- Many corporate organizations, as well as many church ministries, fail to take advantage of workshop experiences. They could benefit from someone to walk beside them as they learn to apply these concepts.

- Action plans, development plans and transformation paths are needed to apply workshop concepts to specific team dynamics and needs.

- After working with a team several times, project champions sometimes e-mail me their team's minutes, and I give feedback and encouragement. This keeps the process moving forward.

- It is important to make sure the team is connected to the organization's overall purpose to keep the team on track. Sometimes the full team "buy in" takes a little longer. A few champions "keeping the dream alive" can provide momentum.

- Find a process coach to come alongside the team for a year or more to serve as an unbiased listener and assist the process development.

- Many workshop participants forget most of what they

heard. However, most of them internalize concepts that are learned and experienced through coaching.

Coaching is the process of pulling their best out of the team members! Coaches express concern, consistency and constancy for the development of the individual and the team. Without coaching, new training concepts and management skills are easily lost. Coaches provide essential tools and encouragement for a team to create a healthy climate and fulfill their compelling purpose, and it lifts the team through challenges and obstacles to the desired future state.

Conclusion

This book has described the basics of team development. While working with groups in this country and Canada, I get many questions about how to begin to develop a team. I hope this book will serve those of you who want to begin this exciting journey.

The best way to use this book is to have each team member read a chapter, sit down together, go over the case study, and answer the discussion questions together. Carve out adequate time for these team discussions because synergy will be found in the midst of your honest and open dialogues. In addition to the leadership team, provide the book for key lay leaders, and guide similar discussions with them. Student groups, college students and other affinity groups will enjoy using the book to stimulate team development discussions. Use the appendices and the reading list to expand your team's knowledge of the development process.

May the Lord bless your team journey and may the effects of team development expand the Kingdom.

CASE STUDY #9

Like most groups without consistent coaching, a large team left a workshop and failed to apply any of the principles they learned because they were immediately engrossed again in their busy schedule.

I had led this team through two workshops on building powerful teams. They interacted, asked questions and participated in the activities. The pastor sat in the front and set a good example by taking notes and asking important questions. Each session was productive, but then, the continuance issue raised its ugly head. I received a call from the project champion telling me the team needed to postpone the rest of the workshop until after the summer, but four months transpired, and I received no call to reschedule the workshop. After reconnecting with the project champion, he informed me that the pastor, the staff and even the champion had lost sight of: (1) the learned concepts, (2) the need to keep the dream alive for team development and (3) the importance of completion. But now, so much time has transpired that the team really needs to start over with the basic concepts.

Discussion Questions

1. Have you seen a team leave a workshop but fail to apply what they learned? What are some reasons this can happen?

2. What are some ways good practices prevent teams from developing best practices? How have you seen this in your experiences?

3. What ways would you try to re-engage this team if you were their coach? List some ways.

4. What importance do you see in team continuation? Describe.

5. What is a good plan of action to attempt with your present team concerning process development? Make an outline of your plan.

ENDNOTES

1. James Surowieki, *The Wisdom of Crowds,* (Doubleday, 2004).
2. Adapted from Pat MacMillan, *The Performance Factor,* (Broadman & Holman, Nashville, 2001), pp. 48-49.
3. www.museum.state.il.us
4. www.saskschools.ca
5. www.riceromp.com
6. MacMillan, *The Performance Factor,* pp. 85-88.
7. Ibid., pp. 88, 96.
8. Sid Kemp, *Project Management Demystified,* (McGraw-Hill Professional, 2004), p. 10.
9. Ibid., p. 11.
10. www.nodakoutdoors.com/snow-goose-migration-2003.php
11. www.saskschools.ca/~gregory/animals/cg/cg8.html
12. Charles Swindoll, *The Tale of the Tardy Oxcart,* (W Publishing Group, Nashville, 1998), p. 476.
13. *Studying Congregations: A New Handbook,* Edited by William McKinney, et al, (Abingdon, Nashville, 1998), p. 132.
14. Ibid., p. 132.
15. Ibid., p. 132.
16. Morgan W. McCall, Jr., *High Flyers,* (Harvard Business School Press, Cambridge, Massachusetts, 1998), pp. 197-198.
17. www.museum.state.il.us.
18. James E. Means, *Leadership in Christian Ministry,* (Grand Rapids: Baker, 1989), p. 113.
19. *The Essential Dictionary of Management and Human Resources,* (New York, Rosenberg: Barnes and Noble Books, 2004), pp. 304, 325.
20. "Contrasts in Prophetic Leadership: Isaiah and Jeremiah," *Biblical Theology Bulletin* (13, no. 2, 1983).

21. John J. Westermann, *The Leadership Continuum*, (Lighthouse Publishing, Deer Lodge, Tennessee, 1997), p. 87.

22. Derric Johnson, *Lists: The Book*, (Y.E.S.S. Publishing, Orlando, 1993), p. 73.

23. Danny Cox, *Leadership When the Heat Is On*, (New York, McGraw-Hill, 1992), pp. 195-196.

24. Ibid., p. 196.

25. Johnson, *Lists: The Book*, p. 74.

26. Kenneth O. Gangel, *Team Leadership in Christian Ministry*, (Moody Press, 1997), pp. 58-59.

27. MacMillan, *The Performance Factor*, p. 123.

28. Ibid., p. 124.

29. Virgil Hurley, *Speaker's Sourcebook of New Illustrations*, (Word Publishing, Dallas, 1995), p. 190.

30. www.saskschools.ca

31. Ed Oakley and Doug Krug, *Enlightened Leadership*, (A Fireside Book, Simon & Schuster, New York, 1991), p. 14.

32. Ibid., p. 96.

33. MacMillan, *The Performance Factor*, pp. 140-148.

34. Ibid., pp. 140-148.

35. www.saskschools.ca

36. Ibid.

37. www.nodakoutdoors.com/snow-goose-migration-2003.php

38. www.saskschools.ca/~gregory/animals

39. Swindoll, *The Tale of the Tardy Oxcart*, p. 99.

40. Ibid., p. 100.

41. *Unger's Bible Dictionary*, (Moody Press, Chicago, 1966), p. 114.

42. Genesis 11:3-4

43. *Halley's Bible Handbook*, (Zondervan, Grand Rapids, Michigan, 1965), p. 83.

44. www.ashland.or.us

45. © 2003-2005 Francois Basili, President, Communication Ideas

Resources

These web sites provide a wealth of information, tools, and other resources from organizations I recommend.

- www.triaxiapartners.com
- www.briefings.com
- www.1to1coachingschool.com
- www.ccl.org
- www.teal.org.uk
- www.cma.org
- www.coaching.com
- www.cpp.com
- www.davidgreenberg.com
- www.growingleaders.com
- www.exed.hbs.edu
- www.coachtrainingalliance.com
- www.adventureassoc.com
- www.theleadershipjourney.org
- www.wiley.com
- www.nextlevelleadership.com
  (Our website has workshops, on-line store, web casts of training and more.)

About Rick Forbus

Rick Forbus has a passion to develop and coach leaders. Holding a doctorate in Human Resource and Leadership Development, Rick has devoted his life to developing visionary leaders of high-performance teams. He is particularly concerned in developing the "inner man" in these leaders and team members.

Since July 2004, Rick has served as the Director of Leadership Initiatives for Next Level Leadership Network conducting workshops, keynote addresses, and retreats for approximately 40,000 participants in the United States, Canada, Kenya, Venezuela, Brazil and Cuba.

Rick speaks nearly every week of the year on topics such as:
- building high-performance teams,
- coaching, leadership greatness,
- communication,
- high-performance meetings,
- decision-making and
- futuring.

He and his wife Nancy have two sons, Maclane and Taylor, and they have two grandsons, Samuel Maclane and Caleb Thompson.

Rick enjoys fly fishing, hunting, gardening, writing, painting with watercolors, and time with his family.

About Next Level Leadership Network

Next Level Leadership Network began in 2000 as a "proof of concept" organization to develop leadership. The first years were spent in finding "clients" from Southern Baptist Convention state leaders, associations and some churches. The initial material and workshops were widely accepted, so more workshops were developed. Today, NLLN has four regional directors, six Master Trainers and many other facilitators conducting workshops, process consulting and coaching in North America. In the last year, 24,200 participants enjoyed some form of NLLN's team development.

NLLN's certified workshop facilitators and process consultants are available to come to your organization and assess, coach and share strategy concepts with you and your team. NLLN works with all types of churches, schools, staff teams, associations and Christian businesses.

NLLN's events range in size from the conference room to the large leadership retreat at a resort or state convention facility. NLLN uses materials on four tracks: (1) team development, (2) diagnostics and assessments, (3) personal development and (4) leadership development. These concepts are presented in a way that is interactive, media-enhanced and with learning activities. The workshops teach the concepts and then a process consultant may come and work with the team in more casual and fluid experiences, guiding and coaching the team to development.

If you or your team is interested in pursuing a strategic team development plan visit the web site www.nextlevel-leadership.com or e-mail Rick at rforbus@namb.net.

TO ORDER MORE COPIES

Migration is designed to help individuals and groups become more effective. Order copies for your friends in business and ministry, and get enough copies for your staff or leadership team. Use the chapters, case studies, and discussion questions to stimulate interaction, insights, and application of the principles in the book.

For more copies…
- Go online to: www.nextlevelleadership.com
- Email: hduke@namb.net or cpage@namb.net
- Call: 888-253-2823 or 770-410-6597
- Write to: Next Level Leadership Network
  4200 North Point Parkway
  Alpharetta, GA 30022

Discounts
$19.95 each
2-8 books: $17.95 each
9-20 books: $16.95 each
Over 20 books:
$14.95 each

Shipping
$3 shipping and handling
$2/book shipping and handling
$1/book shipping and handling

free shipping

Order information
Number of books: _____ at $_____/book = $_____
Shipping: _____ books at $_____/book = $_____
Total: $_____

Payment options
Credit cards are accepted online and by phone. Checks are accepted by mail.